GL(

B|

C000264450

16th edition July 2017

© AA Media Limited 2017

Cartography:
All cartography in this atlas edited, designed and produced by the Mapping Services Department of AA Publishing (A05536).

This atlas contains Ordnance Survey data © Crown copyright and database right 2017 and data from openstreetmap.org © OpenStreetMap Contributors (pages 82–94 only)

Publisher's notes:
Published by AA Publishing (a trading name of AA Media Limited, whose registered office is Fanum House, Basing View, Basingstoke, Hampshire RG21 4EA, UK. Registered number 06112600).

ISBN: 978 0 7495 7880 0 (paperback)

ISBN: 978 0 7495 7879 4 (wire bound)

A CIP Catalogue record for this book is available from the British Library.

Disclaimer:
The contents of this atlas are believed to be correct at the time of the latest revision, it will not contain any subsequent amended, new or temporary information including diversions and traffic control or enforcement systems. The publishers cannot be held responsible or liable for any loss or damage occasioned to any person acting or refraining from action as a result of any use or reliance on material in this atlas, nor for any errors, omissions or changes in such material. This does not affect your statutory rights.

The publishers would welcome information to correct any errors or omissions and to keep this atlas up to date. Please write to the Atlas Editor, AA Publishing, The Automobile Association, Fanum House, Basing View, Basingstoke, Hampshire RG21 4EA, UK.
E-mail: *roadatlasfeedback@theaa.com*

Printer: 1010 Printing International Ltd.

Contents

Map pages	**II**
Atlas symbols	**1**
Road maps of Britain 1:500,000 scale	**2–65**
Index to place names in Britain	**66–80**
County, administrative area map	66–67
Place name index	68–80
Distance charts	**81 & 90**
Britain	81
Ireland	90
Road maps of Ireland 1:1 million scale	**82–89**
Index to place names in Ireland	**91–94**
County, administrative area map	91
Place name index	92–94

Scale 1:500,000
or 8 miles to 1 inch
5km to 1cm

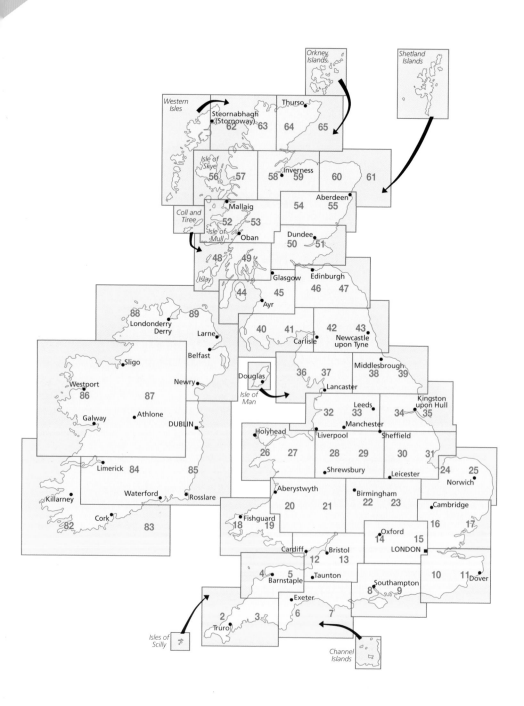

Britain

Motorway with number	M4
Toll motorway with junction	
Motorway junction with and without number	
Restricted motorway junction	
Motorway service area	Fleet
Primary route single/dual carriageway	A40
Primary route junction with and without number	
Restricted primary route junction	
Primary route service area	
Other A road single/dual carriageway	A33
B road	B4224
Unclassified road	
Road tunnel	
Road under construction/approved	

Narrow primary, other A or B road with passing places (Scotland)

Road toll

Distance in miles between symbols

Vehicle ferry

Fast vehicle ferry or catamaran

National boundary

County, administrative boundary

Heliport

Airport

Viewpoint

931
▲
SKIDDAW

Spot height in metres

National Park or National Scenic Area

27 — Page overlap with number

1:500,000   0   5   10 miles   0   5   10   15 kilometres

8 miles to 1 inch

Ireland

Motorway	M1
Toll motorway and plaza	M1 Toll
Motorway junction with and without number	
Restricted motorway junction with and without number	
Motorway service area	Gorey
National primary route (Republic of Ireland)	N7
National secondary route (Republic of Ireland)	N81
Regional road (Republic of Ireland)	R116
Distance in kilometres between symbols (Republic of Ireland)	7
Primary route (Northern Ireland)	A2
A road (Northern Ireland)	A42
B road (Northern Ireland)	B176

Distance in miles between symbols (Northern Ireland)

Minor road

Road tunnel

Road under construction

Vehicle ferry

Fast vehicle ferry or catamaran

International boundary

Airport

Viewpoint

919
▲
Galtymore

Spot height in metres

Gaeltacht (Irish language area)

1:1,000,000   0   10   20 miles   0   10   20   30 kilometres

16 miles to 1 inch

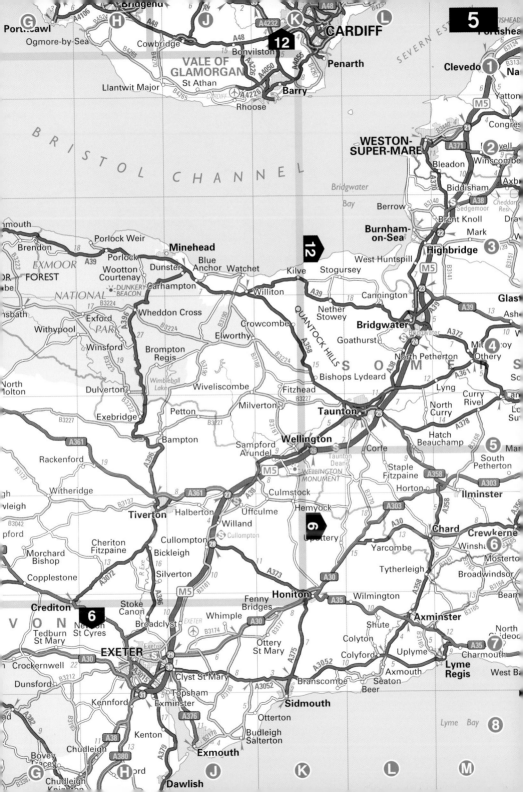

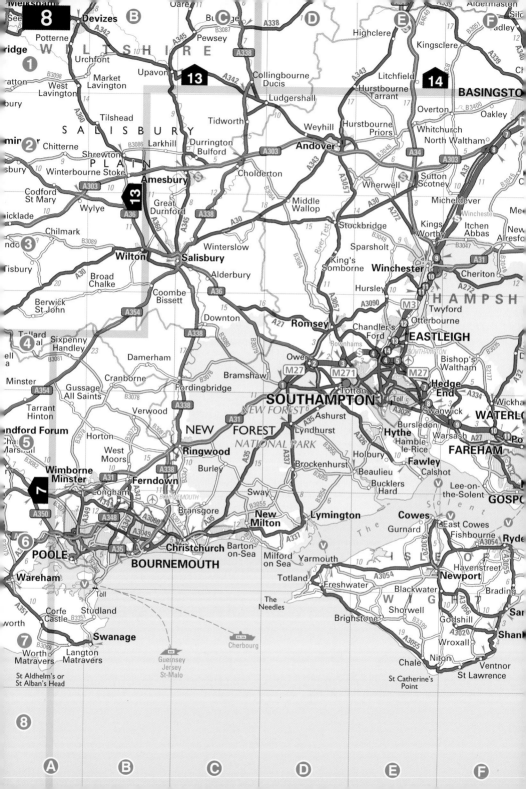

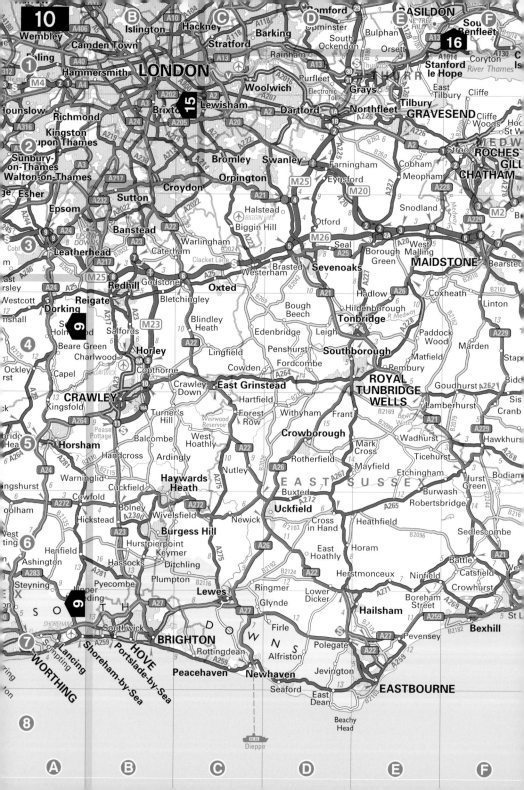

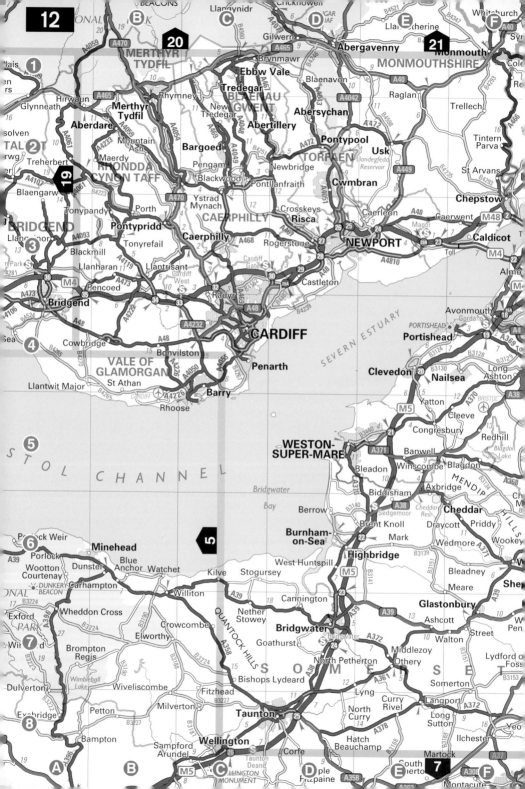

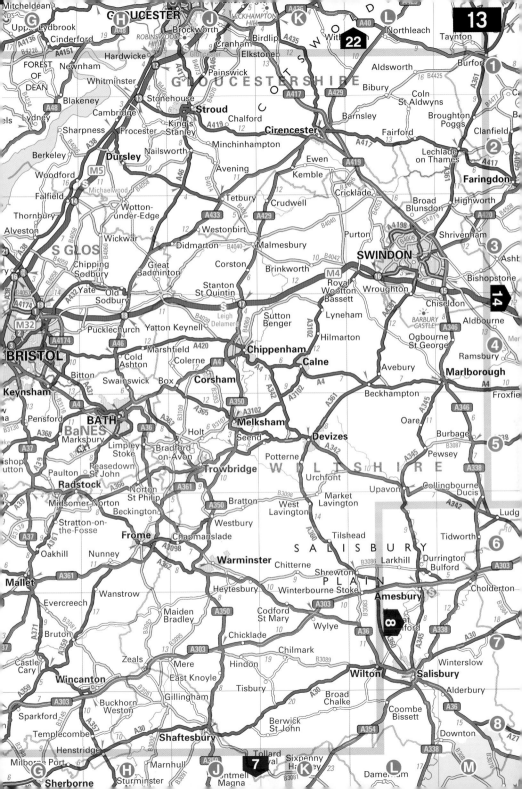

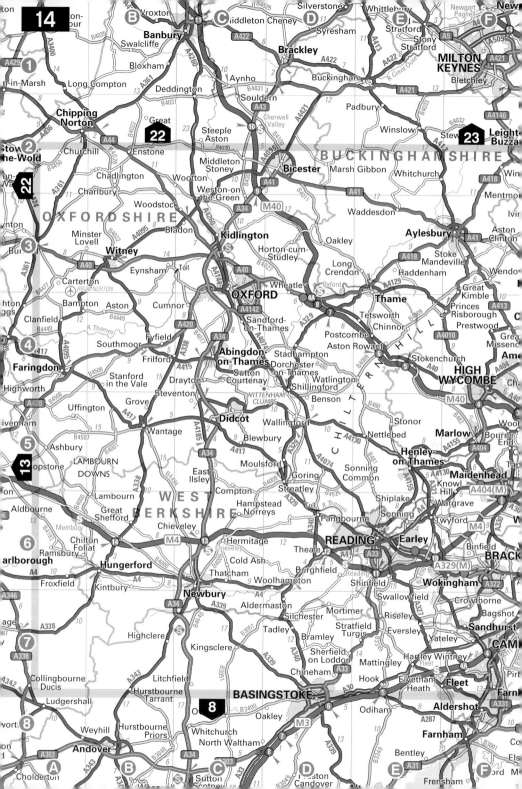

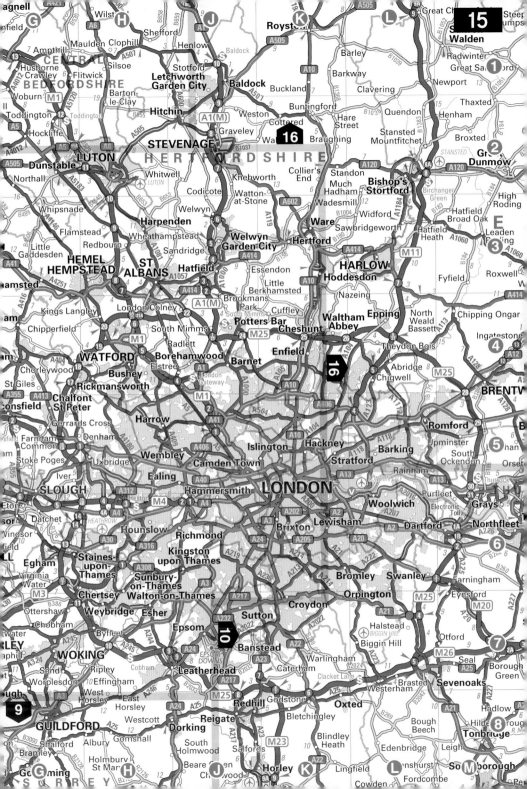

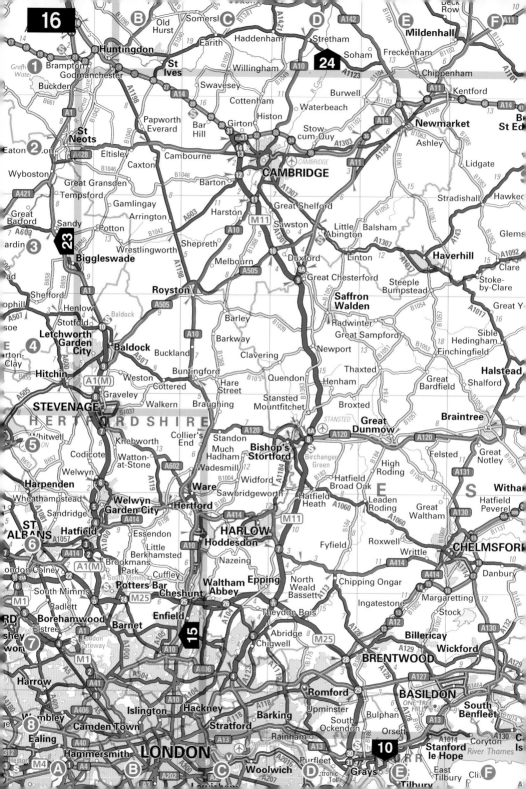

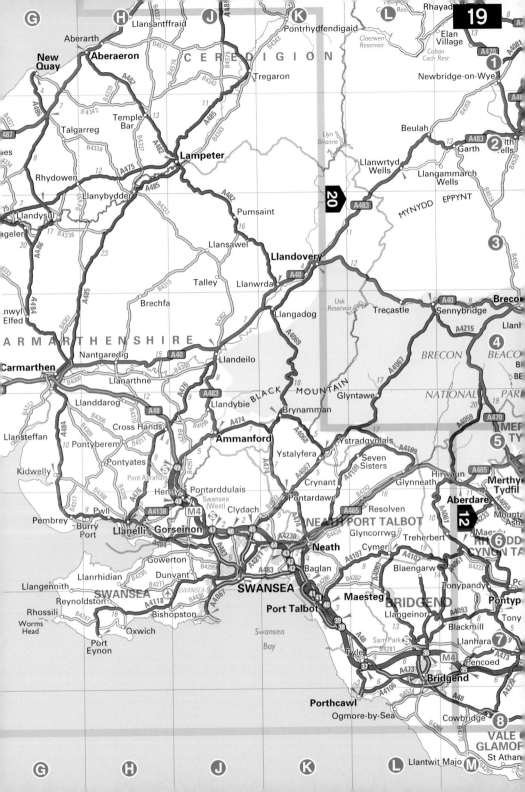

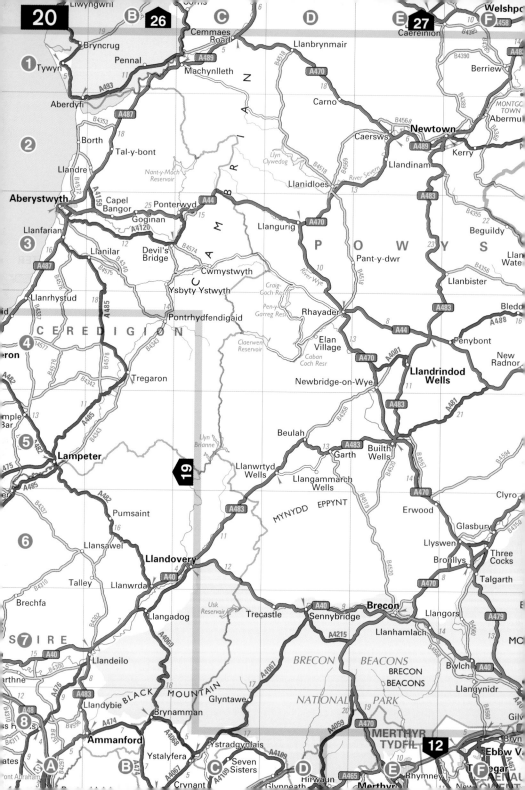

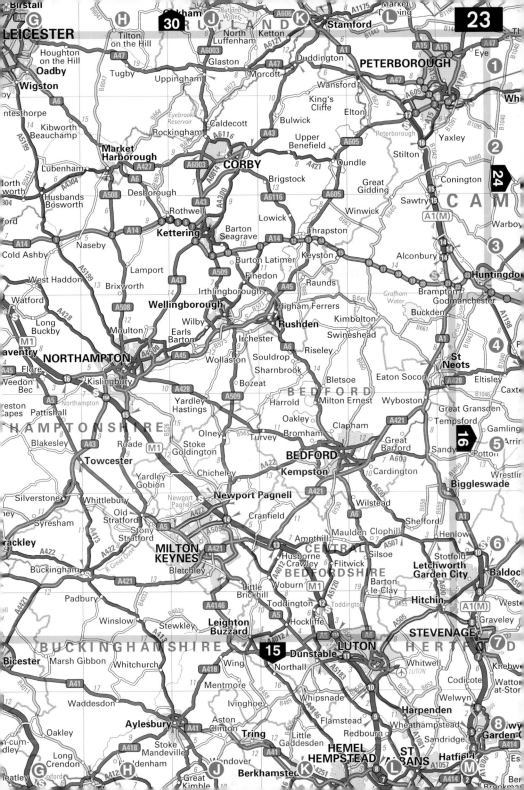

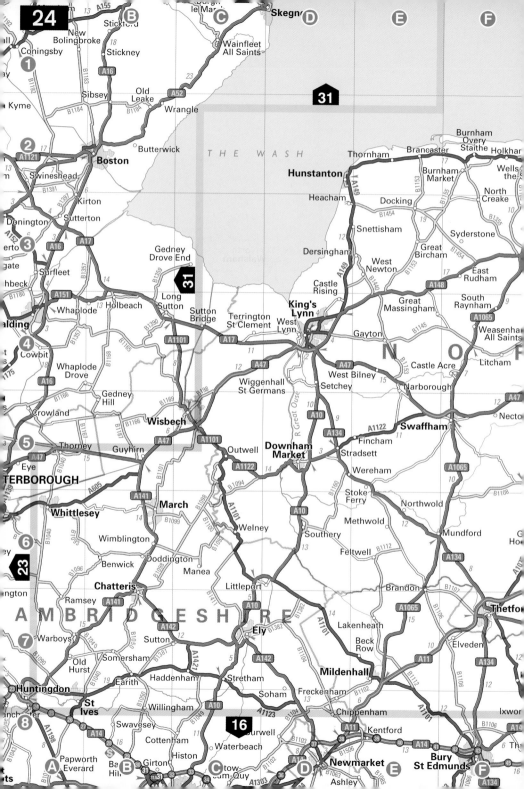

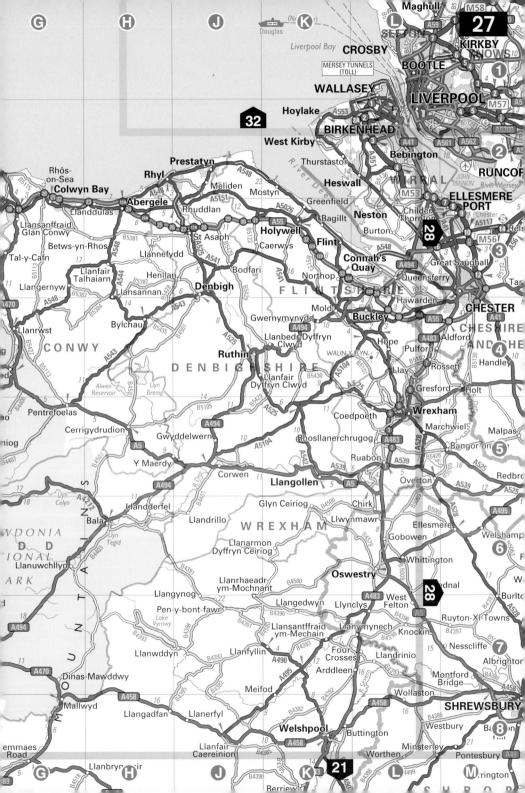

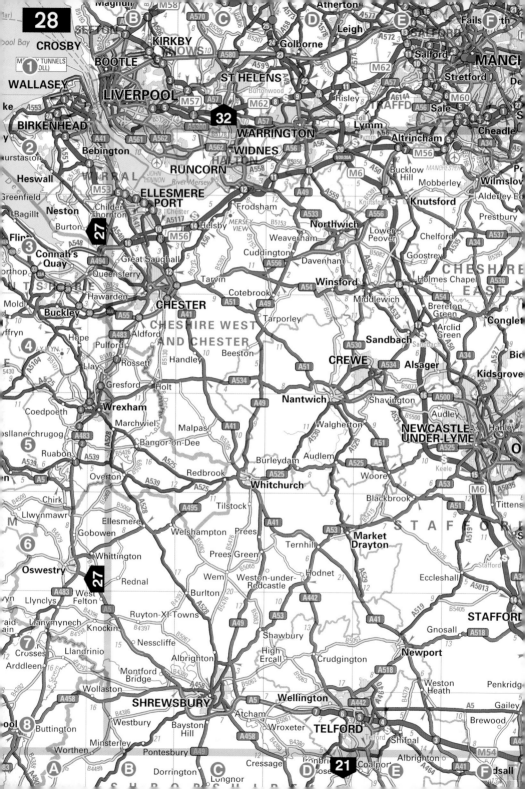

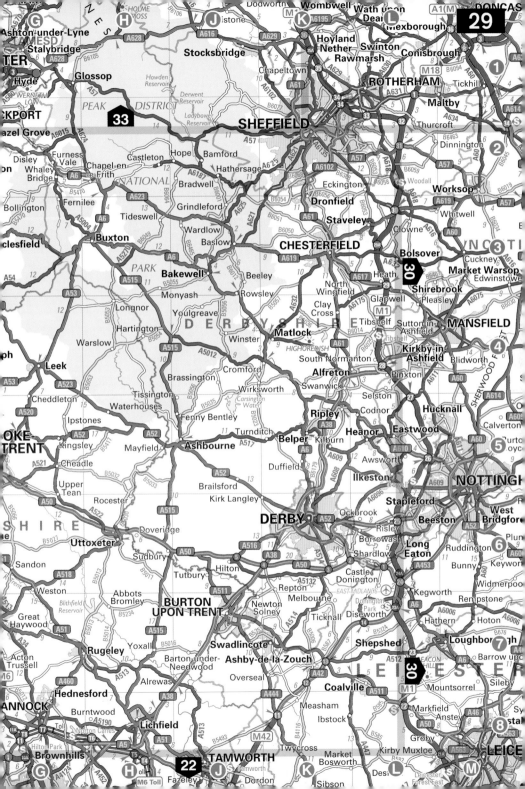

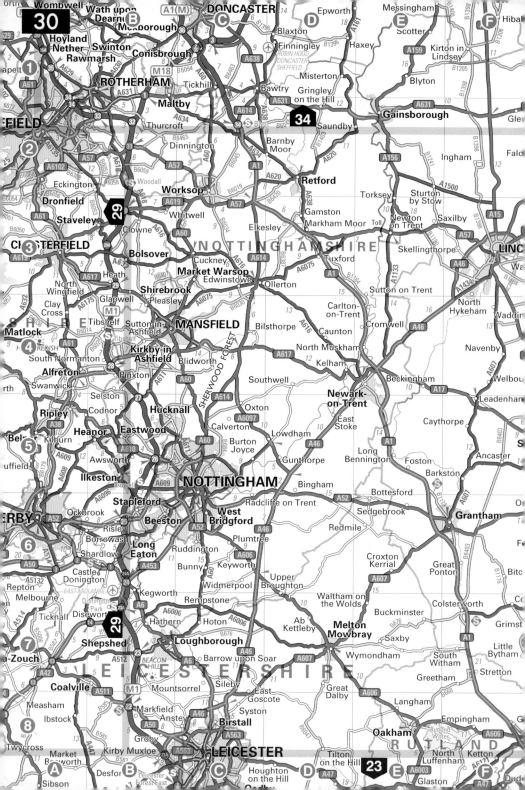

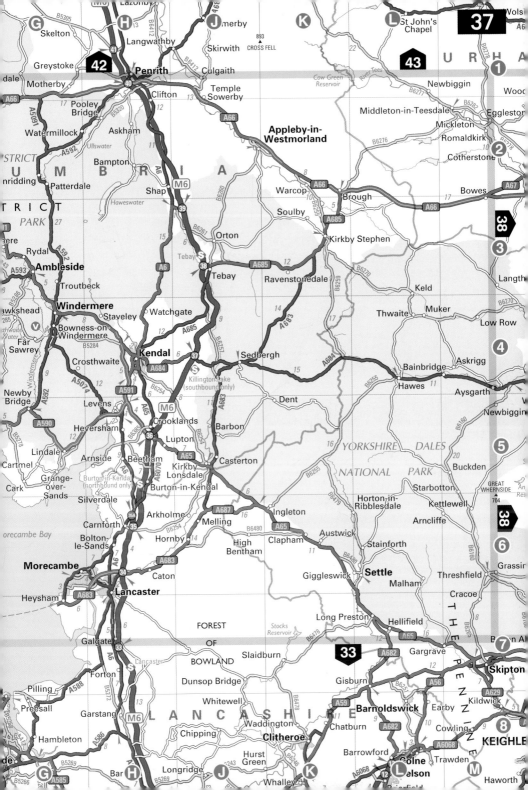

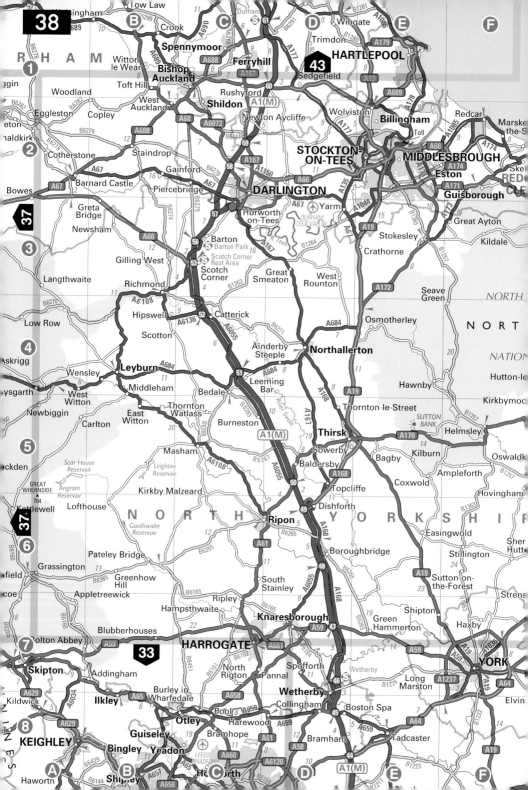

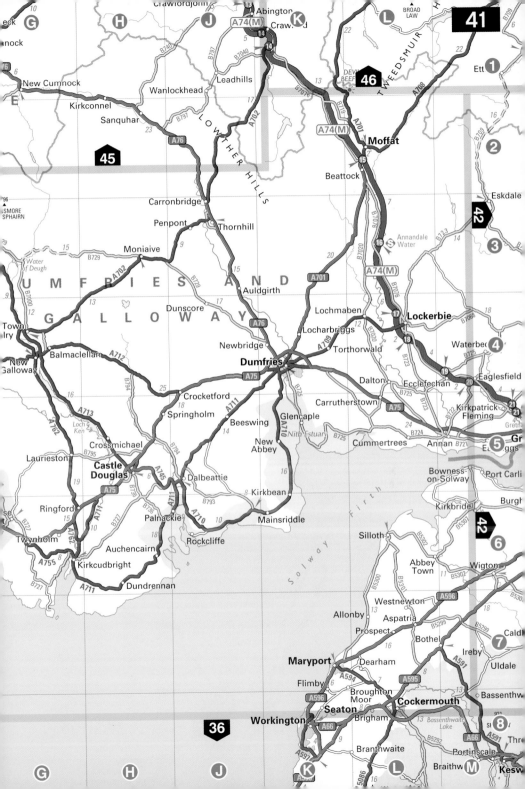

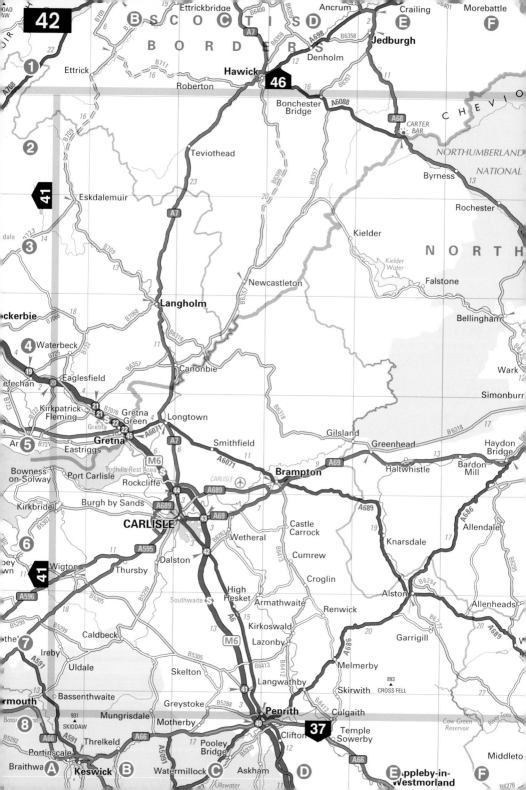

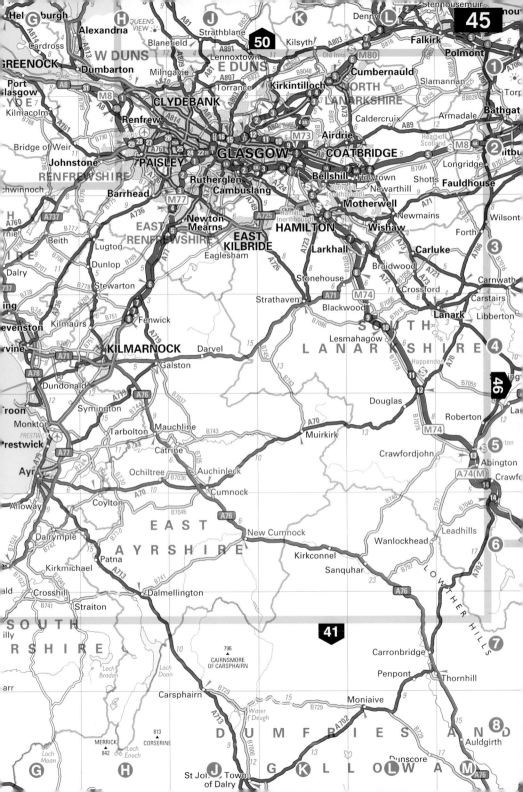

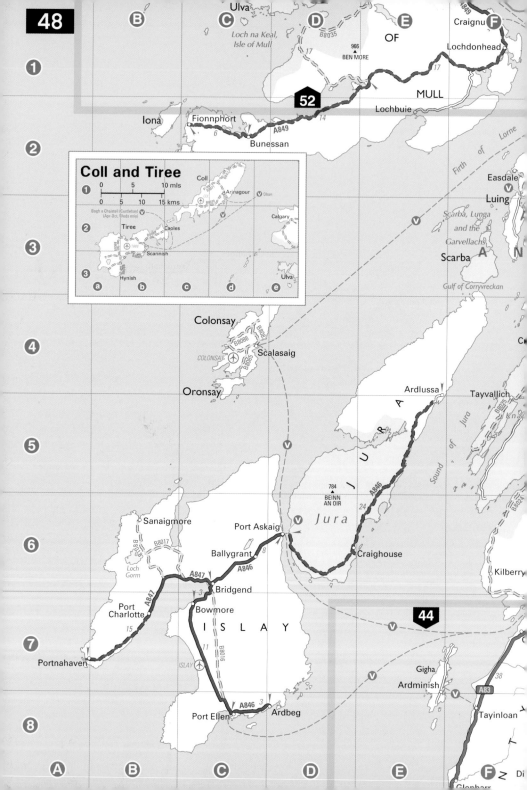

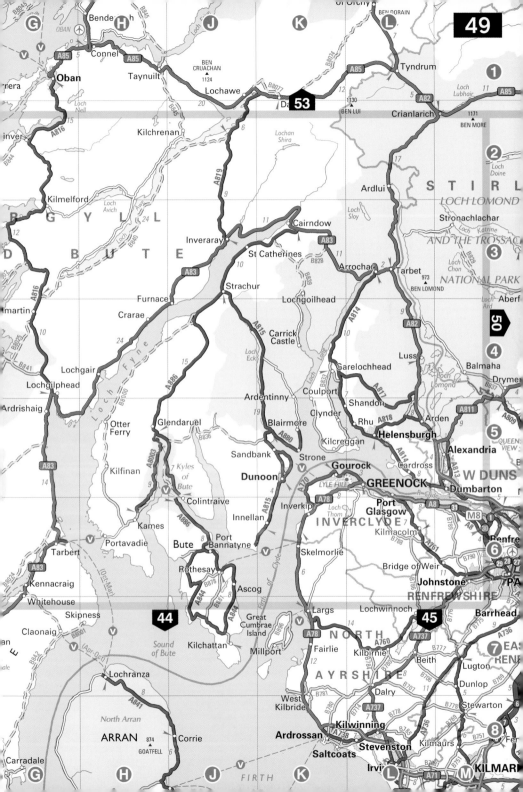

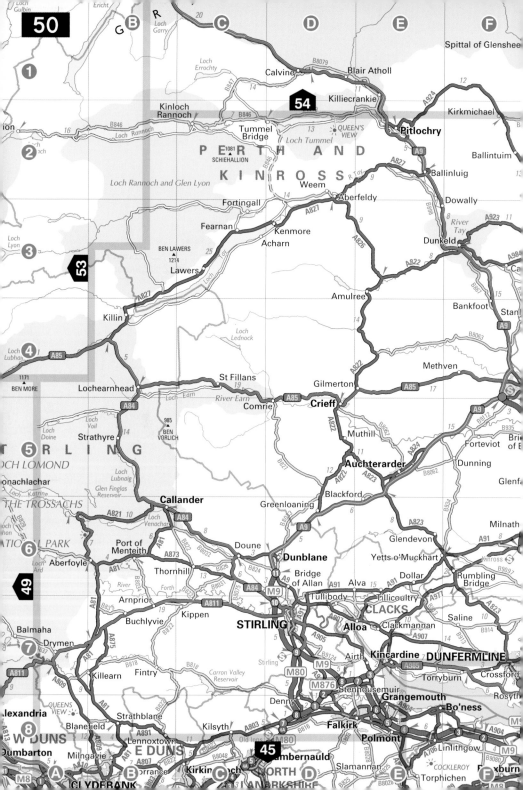

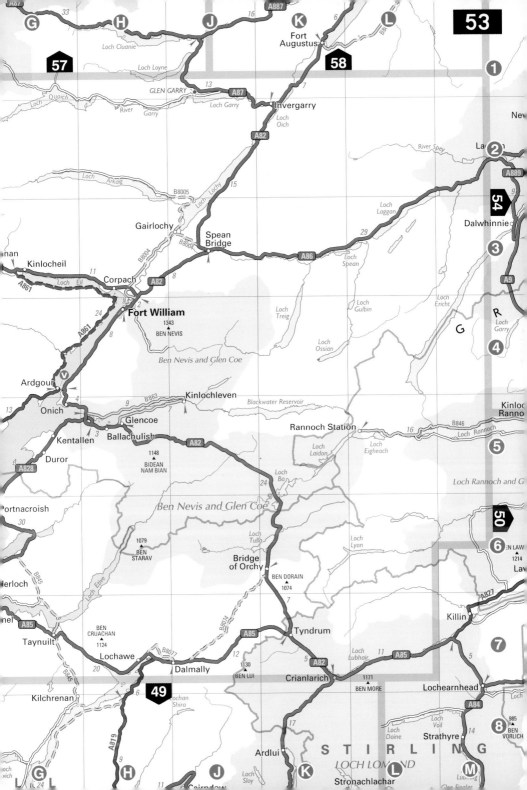

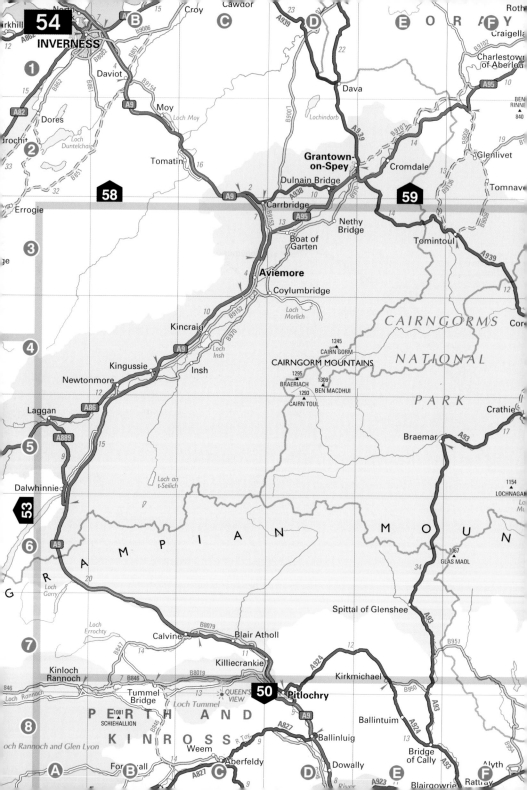

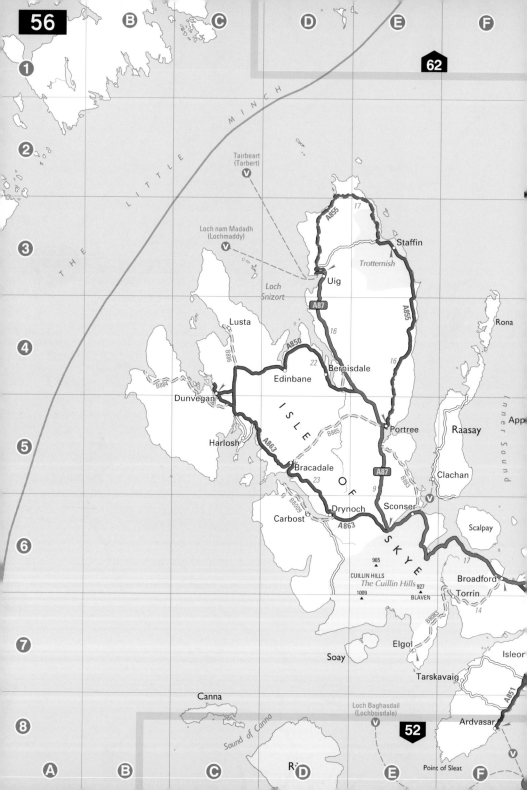

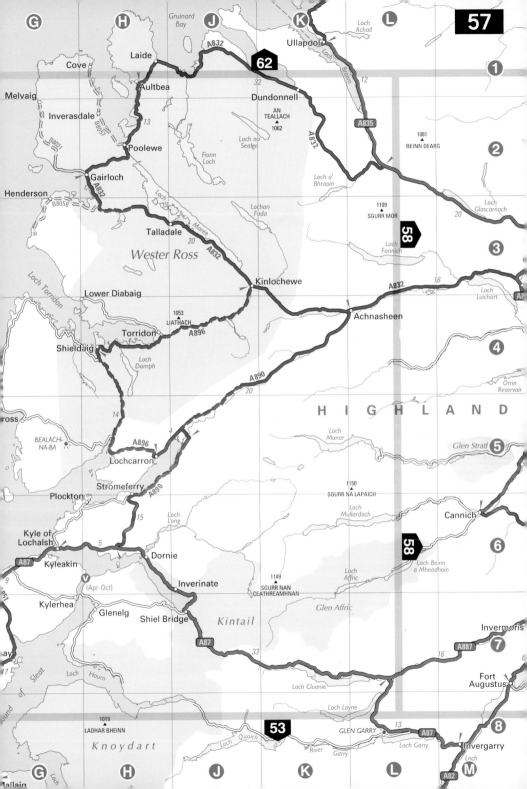

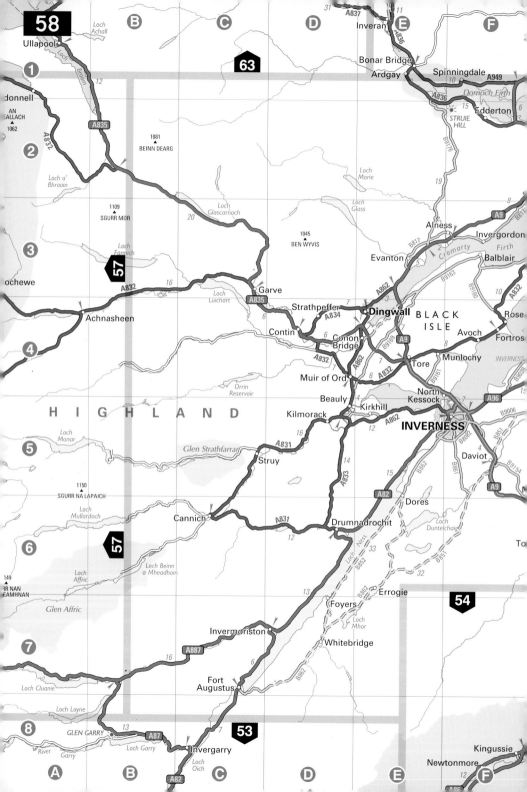

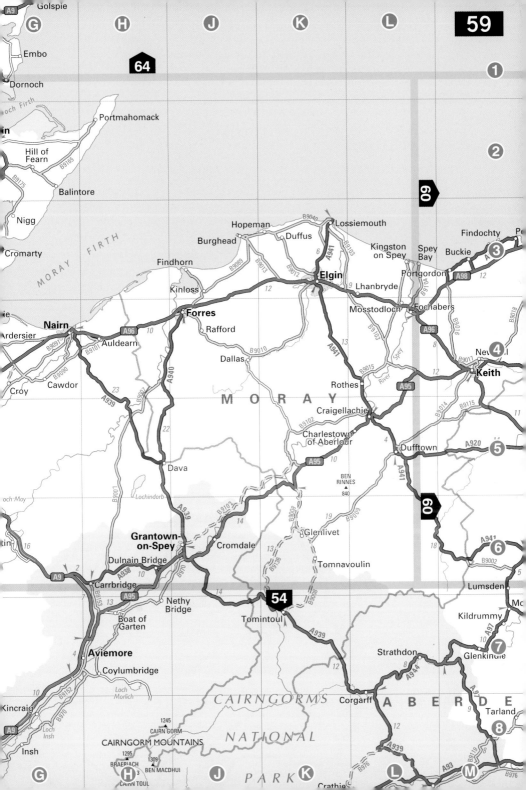

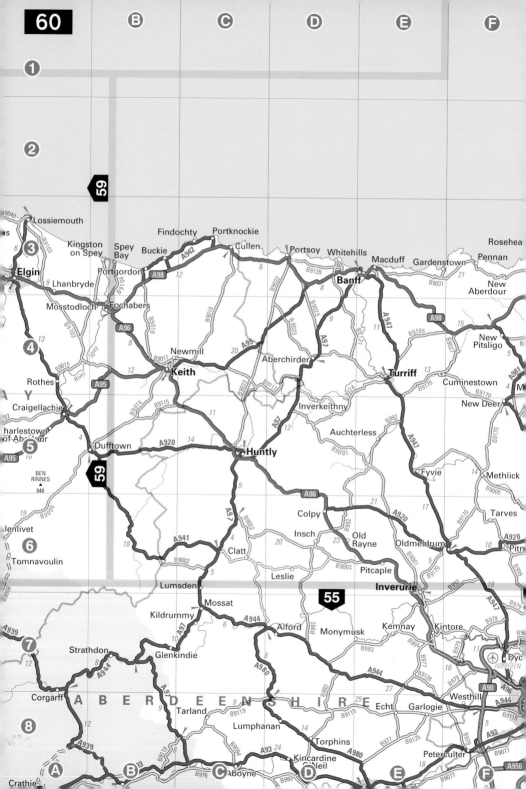

G H J K L M

① ② ③ ④ ⑤ ⑥ ⑦ ⑧

Sandhaven
Fraserburgh
Inverallochy
Memsie
St Combs
Rathen
Crimond
Strichen
St Fergus
Mintlaw
Old Deer
Longside
Peterhead
uartfield
Clola
Boddam
Hatton
Cruden Bay
on
Collieston
den
Newburgh
Balmedie
Kirkwall
Lerwick
ABERDEEN
rtlethen

Shetland Islands

0 5 10 15 mls   *Herma Ness*
0 5 10 15 20 kms

Haroldswick
Unst
Baltasound
Uyeasound
Gutcher
Yell
West
Sandwick
Mid
Yell
Fetlar
Ollaberry
Ulsta
Burravoe
Out
Skerries
Hillswick
Toft
SKERRIES
(Mon, Fri, Sat,
Sun only)
SHETLAND
Brae
Muckle
Roe
Vidlin
Voe
Whalsay
Symbister
ISLANDS
Sandness
(Weds only)
Walls
Lerwick
Kirkabister
Bressay
Foula
(Summer-Tues,
Thurs, Sat only
Winter-Tues,
Thurs only)
Scalloway
Fladdabister
MAINLAND
Sandwick
Kirkwall
Aberdeen
SUMBURGH
Sumburgh
Head
Fair Isle (Summer-Tues,
Thurs, Sat only
Winter-Tues only)

a b c d e

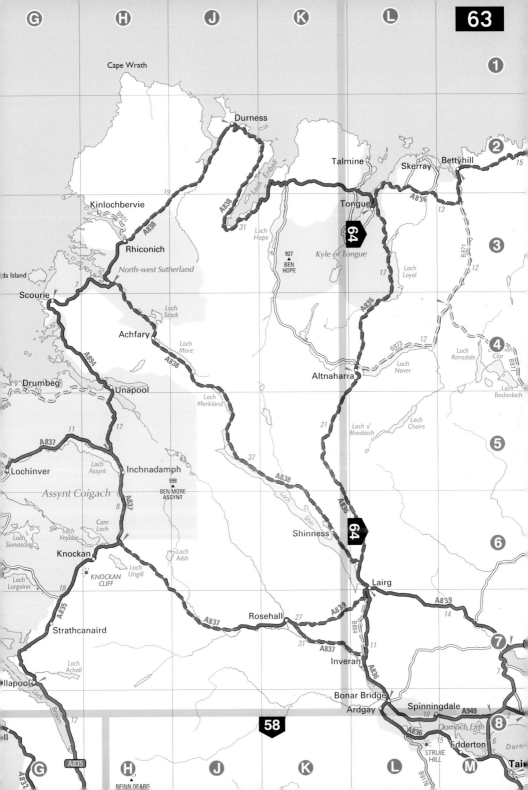

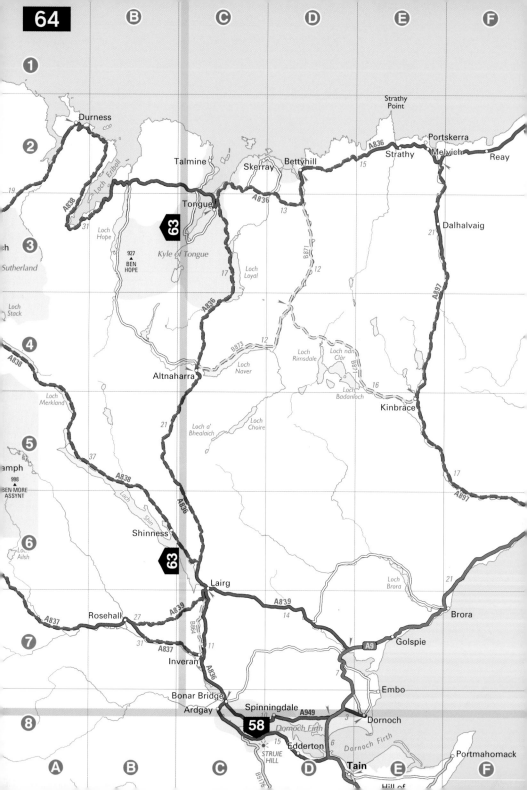

G   H   J   K   L

① ② ③ ④ ⑤ ⑥ ⑦ ⑧

Stromness **V**

Dunnet Head

PENTLAND FIRTH

Island of Stroma

St Margaret's Hope **V**

Duncansby Head

Scrabster

Gills A836 John o' Groats

15

Thurso

Dunnet

Castletown   Freswick

5

Loch Calder

A9   B876   17   A99

Halkirk   B874   16   Keiss

Spittal   A882   Watten   B874

Loch Shurrery   21   A882

Loch More   23   **Wick**

A9   *WICK JOHN O' GROATS*

Thrumster

A9   A99

Latheron   Lybster   17

Dunbeath

Berriedale   20

A9

Helmsdale

Orkney Islands

Mull Head   North Ronaldsay ①

Pierowall   Papa Westray

Westray   **V**   Rapness

Midbea   Sanday

Calfsound   Braeswick ②

Wasbister   Eday   **V** Lerwick

Rousay   *Brough Head*   A966   Backaland

Dounby   ORKNEY   Brinyan   Stronsay

MAINLAND   Hackland   Shapinsay   ③

Finstown   Balfour

A965   **Kirkwall**

Stromness   A964   A960

Houton   St Mary's   Aberdeen ④

HOY   Burray

Rora Head   Lyness   Flotta   St Margaret's Hope

Scrabster **V**   *Scapa Flow*   South Ronaldsay ⑤

V   Burwick

0   5   10 mls

0 5 10 15 kms

PENTLAND FIRTH   ⑥

a Dunnet **b** Gills **c**   **d**

G   H   J   K   L   M

This index lists places appearing in the main-map section of the atlas in alphabetical order. The reference following each name gives the atlas page number and grid reference of the square in which the place appears. The map shows counties, unitary authorities and administrative areas, together with a list of the abbreviated name forms used in the index.

England

BaNES	**Bath & N E Somerset (18)**
Barns	**Barnsley (19)**
Bed	**Bedford**
Birm	**Birmingham**
Bl w D	**Blackburn with Darwen (20)**
Bmouth	**Bournemouth**
Bolton	**Bolton (21)**
Bpool	**Blackpool**
Br & H	**Brighton & Hove (22)**
Br For	**Bracknell Forest (23)**
Bristl	**City of Bristol**
Bucks	**Buckinghamshire**
Bury	**Bury (24)**
C Beds	**Central Bedfordshire**
C Brad	**City of Bradford**
C Derb	**City of Derby**
C KuH	**City of Kingston upon Hull**
C Leic	**City of Leicester**
C Nott	**City of Nottingham**
C Pete	**City of Peterborough**
C Plym	**City of Plymouth**
C Port	**City of Portsmouth**
C Sotn	**City of Southampton**
C Stke	**City of Stoke-on-Trent**
C York	**City of York**
Calder	**Calderdale (25)**
Cambs	**Cambridgeshire**
Ches E	**Cheshire East**
Ches W	**Cheshire West and Chester**
Cnwll	**Cornwall**
Covtry	**Coventry**
Cumb	**Cumbria**
Darltn	**Darlington (26)**
Derbys	**Derbyshire**
Devon	**Devon**
Donc	**Doncaster (27)**
Dorset	**Dorset**
Dudley	**Dudley (28)**
Dur	**Durham**
E R Yk	**East Riding of Yorkshire**
E Susx	**East Sussex**
Essex	**Essex**
Gatesd	**Gateshead (29)**
Gloucs	**Gloucestershire**
Gt Lon	**Greater London**
Halton	**Halton (30)**
Hants	**Hampshire**
Hartpl	**Hartlepool (31)**
Herefs	**Herefordshire**
Herts	**Hertfordshire**
IoS	**Isles of Scilly**
IoW	**Isle of Wight**
Kent	**Kent**
Kirk	**Kirklees (32)**
Knows	**Knowsley (33)**
Lancs	**Lancashire**
Leeds	**Leeds**
Leics	**Leicestershire**
Lincs	**Lincolnshire**
Lpool	**Liverpool**
Luton	**Luton**
M Keyn	**Milton Keynes**
Manch	**Manchester**

Medway	**Medway**
Middsb	**Middlesbrough**
N Linc	**North Lincolnshire**
N Som	**North Somerset (34)**
N Tyne	**North Tyneside (35)**
N u Ty	**Newcastle upon Tyne**
N York	**North Yorkshire**
NE Lin	**North East Lincolnshire**
Nhants	**Northamptonshire**
Norfk	**Norfolk**
Notts	**Nottinghamshire**
Nthumb	**Northumberland**
Oldham	**Oldham (36)**
Oxon	**Oxfordshire**
Poole	**Poole**
R & Cl	**Redcar & Cleveland**
Readg	**Reading**
Rochdl	**Rochdale (37)**
Rothm	**Rotherham (38)**
Rutlnd	**Rutland**
S Glos	**South Gloucestershire (39)**
S on T	**Stockton-on-Tees (40)**
S Tyne	**South Tyneside (41)**
Salfd	**Salford (42)**
Sandw	**Sandwell (43)**
Sefton	**Sefton (44)**
Sheff	**Sheffield**
Shrops	**Shropshire**
Slough	**Slough (45)**
Solhll	**Solihull (46)**
Somset	**Somerset**
St Hel	**St Helens (47)**
Staffs	**Staffordshire**
Sthend	**Southend-on-Sea**
Stockp	**Stockport (48)**
Suffk	**Suffolk**
Sundld	**Sunderland**
Surrey	**Surrey**
Swindn	**Swindon**
Tamesd	**Tameside (49)**
Thurr	**Thurrock (50)**
Torbay	**Torbay**
Traffd	**Trafford (51)**
W & M	**Windsor and Maidenhead (52)**
W Berk	**West Berkshire**
W Susx	**West Sussex**
Wakefd	**Wakefield (53)**
Warrtn	**Warrington (54)**
Warwks	**Warwickshire**
Wigan	**Wigan (55)**
Wilts	**Wiltshire**
Wirral	**Wirral (56)**
Wokham	**Wokingham (57)**
Wolves	**Wolverhampton (58)**
Worcs	**Worcestershire**
Wrekin	**Telford & Wrekin (59)**
Wsall	**Walsall (60)**

Channel Islands & Isle of Man

Guern	**Guernsey**
Jersey	**Jersey**
IoM	**Isle of Man**

Scotland

Abers	**Aberdeenshire**
Ag & B	**Argyll and Bute**
Angus	**Angus**
Border	**Scottish Borders**
C Aber	**City of Aberdeen**
C Dund	**City of Dundee**
C Edin	**City of Edinburgh**
C Glas	**City of Glasgow**
Clacks	**Clackmannanshire (1)**
D & G	**Dumfries & Galloway**
E Ayrs	**East Ayrshire**
E Duns	**East Dunbartonshire (2)**
E Loth	**East Lothian**
E Rens	**East Renfrewshire (3)**
Falk	**Falkirk**
Fife	**Fife**
Highld	**Highland**
Inver	**Inverclyde (4)**
Mdloth	**Midlothian (5)**
Moray	**Moray**
N Ayrs	**North Ayrshire**
N Lans	**North Lanarkshire (6)**
Ork	**Orkney Islands**
P & K	**Perth & Kinross**
Rens	**Renfrewshire (7)**
S Ayrs	**South Ayrshire**
S Lans	**South Lanarkshire**
Shet	**Shetland Islands**
Stirlg	**Stirling**
W Duns	**West Dunbartonshire (8)**
W Isls	**Western Isles (Na h-Eileanan an Iar)**
W Loth	**West Lothian**

Wales

Blae G	**Blaenau Gwent (9)**
Brdgnd	**Bridgend (10)**
Caerph	**Caerphilly (11)**
Cardif	**Cardiff**
Carmth	**Carmarthenshire**
Cerdgn	**Ceredigion**
Conwy	**Conwy**
Denbgs	**Denbighshire**
Flints	**Flintshire**
Gwynd	**Gwynedd**
IoA	**Isle of Anglesey**
Mons	**Monmouthshire**
Myr Td	**Merthyr Tydfil (12)**
Neath	**Neath Port Talbot (13)**
Newpt	**Newport (14)**
Pembks	**Pembrokeshire**
Powys	**Powys**
Rhondd	**Rhondda Cynon Taff (15)**
Swans	**Swansea**
Torfn	**Torfaen (16)**
V Glam	**Vale of Glamorgan (17)**
Wrexhm	**Wrexham**

ORKNEY ISLANDS

SHETLAND ISLANDS

WESTERN ISLES (Na h-Eileanan an Iar)

HIGHLAND

MORAY

Aberdeen

S C O T L A N D

ABERDEENSHIRE

ANGUS

PERTH & KINROSS

Dundee

ARGYLL AND BUTE

STIRLING

FIFE

1

FALK

Edinburgh

W LOTH

E LOTH

8 2

4 Glasgow

7 6

3 5

NORTH AYRSHIRE

S LANS

SCOTTISH BORDERS

E AYRS

S AYRS

DUMFRIES & GALLOWAY

NORTHUMBERLAND

Newcastle upon Tyne 35

29 41

Sunderland

CUMBRIA

DURHAM 31

26 40 R & CL

Middlesbrough

IoM

NORTH YORKSHIRE

Blackpool

Bradford

York

EAST RIDING OF YORKSHIRE

LANCASHIRE

25

Leeds

Kingston upon Hull

20

53

N LINC

NE LIN

21 24 37

32

19

27

44

55 36

33 47 42 49

Manchester

38

Liverpool

56 54 51 48

Sheffield

IoA

30

LINCOLNSHIRE

CONWY

FLINTS

CHES W

CHES E

DERBYS

NOTTS

DENBGS

Stoke-on-Trent

WREXHAM

Derby

Nottingham

GWYNEDD

STAFFS

LEICS

RUTLAND

59

Peterborough

NORFOLK

SHROPSHIRE

58 60

LEICester

POWYS

28 43

Birmingham

46 Coventry

NHANTS

CAMBS

SUFFOLK

CERDGN

WORCS

WARWKS

Milton Keynes

BED

HEREFS

W A L E S

E N G L A N D

PEMBKS

CARMTH

GLOUCS

OXON

BUCKS

BEDS Luton

HERTS

ESSEX

12 9

MONS

13 16

Swansea

15 11 14

10 Cardiff

17

Bristol

39

Swindon

Reading 52 45

W BERK 57 23

GREATER LONDON

50

Southend-on-Sea

MEDWAY

34 18

WILTSHIRE

SURREY

KENT

SOMERSET

HAMPSHIRE

W SUSX

E SUSX

22

DEVON

DORSET

Southampton

Portsmouth

Bournemouth

Poole

IoW

CORNWALL

Plymouth

Torbay

GUERNSEY

CHANNEL ISLANDS

JERSEY

IoS

A

Abberley Worcs 21 L4
Abbey Town Cumb 41 L6
Abbots Bromley
   Staffs 29 H7
Aberaeron Cerdgn ... 19 H1
Aberarth Cerdgn 19 H1
Aberchirder Abers 60 D4
Aberdare Rhondd 12 B2
Aberdaron Gwynd 26 B6
Aberdeen C Aber 55 M4
Aberdyfi IoA 20 A2
Aberfeldy P & K 50 D2
Aberffraw IoA 26 C3
Aberfoyle Stirlg 50 B6
Abergavenny Mons ... 21 G8
Abergele Conwy 27 H3
Aberlady E Loth 46 E2
Aberlour,
   Charlestown of
   Moray 59 L5
Abermule Powys 20 F2
Abernethy P & K 51 G5
Aberporth Cerdgn ... 18 F2
Abersoch Gwynd 26 C6
Abersychan Torfn 12 D2
Abertillery Blae G 12 D2
Aberystwyth Cerdgn... 20 A3
Abingdon-on-
   Thames Oxon 14 C4
Abington S Lans 45 M5
Ab Kettleby Leics 30 D7
Aboyne Abers 55 J4
Abridge Essex 16 D7
Accrington Lancs 33 G4
Acharacle Highld 52 D4
Acharn P & K 50 C3
Achfary Highld 63 H4
Achiltibuie Highld 62 F6
Achnacroish Ag & B... 52 F6
Achnasheen Highld... 57 L4
Ackworth Moor Top
   Wakefd 34 B5
Acle Norfk 25 K5
Acton Trussell Staffs... 29 G7
Addingham C Brad.... 33 J2
Adwick le Street
   Donc 34 C6
Ainderby Steeple
   N York 38 D4
Airdrie N Lans 45 L2
Airth Falk 50 E7
Albrighton Shrops ... 21 L1
Albrighton Shrops ... 28 C7
Albury Surrey 9 K2
Alcester Warwks 22 B4
Alconbury Cambs 23 M3
Aldbourne Wilts 14 A6
Aldbrough E R Yk 35 J3
Aldeburgh Suffk 17 M2
Alderbury Wilts 8 C3
Alderley Edge Ches E... 28 F3
Aldermaston W Berk... 14 D7
Alderminster Warwks... 22 D5
Aldershot Hants 9 H2
Aldford Ches W 28 B4
Aldham Essex 17 G5
Aldsworth Gloucs 13 L1
Alexandria W Duns ... 49 M5
Alfold Surrey 9 K3
Alford Abers 55 J3
Alford Lincs 31 K3
Alfreton Derbys 29 L4
Alfriston E Susx 10 D7
Alkham Kent 11 K4
Allanton Border 47 H4
Allendale Nthumb 42 F6
Allenheads Nthumb... 42 F7
Allensmore Herefs ... 21 J6
Alloa Clacks 50 E7
Allonby Cumb 41 L7
Almondsbury S Glos... 13 G3
Alness Highld 58 F3
Alnmouth Nthumb ... 43 K2
Alnwick Nthumb 47 L7
Airewas Staffs 29 J7
Alsager Ches E 28 E4
Alston Cumb 42 E6
Altandhu Highld 62 F6
Althorpe N Linc 34 E5
Altnaharra Highld 64 C4
Alton Hants 9 G2
Alton Pancras Dorset... 7 K2
Altrincham Traffd 28 E2
Alva Clacks 50 E6
Alveston S Glos 13 G3
Alyth P & K 51 G3
Amberley W Susx 9 K4
Amble Nthumb 43 K2

Ambleside Cumb......... 37 G3
Amersham Bucks 15 L4
Amesbury Wilts 8 C2
Amlwch IoA 26 D1
Ammanford Carmth... 19 J5
Ampleforth N York.... 38 F5
Ampthill C Beds 23 K6
Amroth Pembks 18 E5
Amulree P & K........... 50 E3
Ancaster Lincs 30 F5
Ancroft Nthumb 47 K5
Ancrum Border 47 G7
Andover Hants 8 D2
Andoversford Gloucs... 22 B7
Andreas IoM 36 C1
Angle Pembks 18 C6
Angmering W Susx..... 9 K5
Annan D & G 41 M5
Annfield Plain Dur 43 J6
Anstey Leics 30 C8
Anstruther Fife 51 K6
An t-Ob W Isls 62 e7
Anwick Lincs 31 G5
Appleby-in-
   Westmorland
   Cumb 37 J2
Applecross Highld ... 57 G5
Appledore Devon 4 D4
Appledore Kent 11 H5
Appletreewick
   N York 38 A7
Arbroath Angus 51 L3
Arclid Green Ches E... 28 E4
Ardbeg Ag & B 48 D8
Arddleen Powys 27 L7
Arden Ag & B 49 L5
Ardentinny Ag & B.... 49 K4
Ardersier Highld 59 G4
Ardgay Highld 64 C8
Ardgour Highld 53 G4
Ardingly W Susx 10 C5
Ardleigh Essex 17 H4
Ardlui Ag & B 49 L2
Ardlussa Ag & B........ 48 C4
Arduaine Ag & B 48 C4
Ardminish Ag & B 44 A3
Ardrishaig Ag & B 49 G5
Ardrossan N Ayrs...... 44 F4
Ardvasar Highld 52 D7
Ardwell D & G 40 C7
Arinagour Ag & B 48 d1
Arisaig Highld 52 D3
Arkholme Lancs 37 J6
Armadale W Loth 45 M2
Armathwaite Cumb... 42 C7
Arncliffe N York 37 M6
Arnside Cumb 37 H5
Arrington Cambs 16 B3
Arrochar Ag & B 49 L3
Arundel W Susx 9 K5
Ascog Ag & B 49 J6
Ascot W & M 15 G6
Ash Kent 11 K3
Ashbourne Derbys ... 29 J5
Ashburton Devon 6 B5
Ashbury Oxon 14 A5
Ashby-de-la-Zouch
   Leics 29 K7
Ashcott Somset 12 E7
Ashford Kent 11 H4
Ashington Nthumb.... 43 K3
Ashington W Susx 9 L4
Ashley Cambs 16 E2
Ashton-under-Lyne
   Tamesd 33 H6
Ashurst Hants 8 D5
Ashwater Devon 4 D7
Askam in Furness
   Cumb 36 F5
Askern Donc 34 C5
Askham Cumb 37 H2
Askrigg N York 37 M4
Aspatria Cumb 41 L7
Aston Oxon 14 B4
Aston Clinton Bucks ... 14 F3
Aston on Clun Shrops... 21 H3
Aston Rowant Oxon... 14 E4
Atcham Shrops 28 C8
Atherstone Warwks ... 22 D1
Atherton Wigan 32 F6
Attleborough Norfk... 25 H6
Attlebridge Norfk 25 H4
Atwick E R Yk 35 H2
Auchenblae Abers 55 K6
Auchencairn D & G ... 41 H6
Auchinleck E Ayrs 45 J5
Auchterarder P & K... 50 E6
Auchterless Abers 60 E5
Auchtermuchty Fife... 51 G5
Audlem Ches E 28 D5
Audley Staffs 28 E5
Auldearn Highld 59 H4

Auldgirth D & G......... 41 J3
Aultbea Highld.......... 57 H1
Austwick N York 37 K6
Avebury Wilts............ 13 L4
Avening Gloucs 13 J2
Aveton Gifford
   Devon 6 A6
Aviemore Highld 54 C3
Avoch Highld............ 58 F4
Avonmouth Bristl 12 F4
Awsworth Notts........ 30 B5
Axbridge Somset...... 12 E5
Axminster Devon 6 F3
Axmouth Devon 6 F3
Aylesbury Bucks 14 F3
Aylesham Kent 11 K3
Aylsham Norfk 25 J3
Aynho Nhants 22 F6
Ayr S Ayrs 45 G5
Aysgarth N York 38 A4
Ayton Border 47 J4

B

Backaland Ork.......... 65 d2
Bacton Norfk 25 K3
Bacup Lancs 33 H4
Bagby N York 38 E5
Bagh a Chaisteil
   W Isls...................... 62 b14
Bagillt Flints 27 K3
Bagnan Neath 19 K6
Bagshot Surrey......... 14 F7
Baile Ailein W Isls..... 62 g4
Baile a Mhanaich
   W Isls...................... 62 C10
Bainbridge N York.... 37 M4
Bainton E R Yk 34 F2
Bakewell Derbys....... 29 J3
Bala Gwynd............... 27 H6
Balallan W Isls 62 g4
Balbeggie P & K........ 51 G4
Balblair Highld 58 F3
Balcombe W Susx 10 B5
Baldersby N York 38 D5
Baldock Herts 16 B4
Balerno C Edin.......... 46 C3
Balfour Ork 65 c3
Balintore Highld 59 G2
Balivanich W Isls...... 62 C10
Ballachulish Highld... 53 H5
Ballantrae S Ayrs 40 B4
Ballasalla IoM 36 b4
Ballater Abers 55 G5
Ballaugh IoM 36 c2
Ballinluig P & K 50 E2
Ballintuim P & K 50 F2
Ballygrant Ag & B 48 C6
Balmaclellan D & G ... 41 G4
Balmaha Stirlg.......... 49 M4
Balmedie Abers 55 M3
Balsall Common Solhll... 22 D3
Balsham Cambs 16 D2
Baltasound Shet 61 d1
Bamber Bridge Lancs... 32 E4
Bamburgh Nthumb ... 47 L6
Bamford Derbys 29 J2
Bampton Cumb 37 H2
Bampton Devon 5 H5
Bampton Oxon 14 A4
Banbury Oxon 22 E6
Banchory Abers 55 K5
Banff Abers 60 E3
Bangor Gwynd.......... 26 E3
Bangor-on-Dee
   Wrexhm 28 B5
Banham Norfk 25 H6
Bankfoot P & K 50 F4
Banstead Surrey....... 10 B3
Banwell N Som 12 E5
Barabhas W Isls 62 h2
Barbon Cumb 37 J5
Bardney Lincs........... 31 G3
Bardon Mill Nthumb... 42 F5
Bardsea Cumb 36 F5
Barford Warwks........ 22 D4
Bargoed Caerph 12 C2
Bar Hill Cambs 16 C2
Barking Gt Lon......... 16 D4
Barkston Lincs 30 F5
Barkway Herts.......... 16 C4
Barley Herts 16 C4
Barmby Moor E R Yk... 34 E2
Barmouth Gwynd 26 E7
Barmston E R Yk 39 L7
Barnard Castle Dur... 38 A2
Barnby Moor Notts... 30 D2
Barnet Gt Lon 15 J4
Barnetby le Wold
   N Linc..................... 35 G6

Barnoldswick Lancs... 33 H3
Barnsley Barns......... 33 M6
Barnsley Gloucs 13 L2
Barnstaple Devon 4 E4
Barr S Ayrs 40 D3
Barrasford Nthumb... 43 G4
Barrhead E Rens....... 45 H3
Barrhill S Ayrs 40 D4
Barrowford Lancs..... 33 H3
Barrow-in-Furness
   Cumb 36 E6
Barrow upon Soar
   Leics 30 C7
Barry V Glam 5 K1
Barton Cambs 16 C2
Barton Lancs 32 E3
Barton N York 38 C3
Barton-le-Clay
   C Beds 23 L7
Barton-on-Sea Hants... 8 C6
Barton Seagrave
   Nhants 23 J3
Barton-under-
   Needwood Staffs... 29 J7
Barton-upon-
   Humber N Linc 35 G5
Barvas W Isls 62 h2
Barwell Leics 22 E2
Basildon Essex 16 F7
Basingstoke Hants 9 G1
Baslow Derbys 29 J3
Bassenthwaite
   Cumb 42 A8
Baston Lincs 31 G7
Bath BaNES 13 H5
Bathgate W Loth 46 A3
Batley Kirk 33 L4
Battle E Susx 10 F6
Baumber Lincs 31 H3
Bawdeswell Norfk 25 H4
Bawdsey Suffk 17 L4
Bawtry Donc 34 D7
Baycliff Cumb 36 F6
Bayston Hill Shrops... 28 C8
Beaconsfield Bucks... 15 G5
Beadnell Nthumb..... 47 L6
Beaford Devon 4 E5
Beal Nthumb 47 K5
Beaminster Dorset.... 7 H2
Beare Green Surrey.... 9 L2
Bearsted Kent.......... 10 F3
Beattock D & G 41 L2
Beaulieu Hants.......... 8 E5
Beauly Highld........... 58 D5
Beaumaris IoA.......... 26 E3
Beaumont Jersey 7 b2
Beaworthy Devon 4 D7
Bebington Wirral...... 27 L2
Beccles Suffk 25 L6
Beckhampton Wilts ... 13 L4
Beckingham Lincs.... 30 E4
Beckington Somset... 13 H6
Beck Row Suffk 24 E7
Bedale N York 38 C4
Beddgelert Gwynd ... 26 E5
Bedford Bed 23 K5
Bedlington Nthumb... 43 K4
Bedworth Warwks 22 E2
Beeford E R Yk 35 H2
Beeley Derbys 29 J3
Beer Devon 6 F3
Beesands Devon 6 B7
Beeston Ches W 28 C4
Beeston Notts 30 B6
Beeswing D & G........ 41 J5
Beetham Cumb 37 H5
Beetley Norfk 25 G4
Beguildy Powys 20 F3
Beith N Ayrs 45 G3
Belford Nthumb........ 47 L6
Bellingham Nthumb... 42 F4
Bellochantuy Ag & B... 44 A5
Bellshill N Lans 45 K2
Belper Derbys 29 K5
Belsay Northumb 43 H4
Belton N Linc 34 E6
Belton Norfk 25 L5
Bembridge IoW 9 G6
Bempton E R Yk 39 L6
Benderloch Ag & B ... 52 F6
Benenden Kent 10 F5
Benllech IoA 26 D2
Benson Oxon 14 D5
Bentley Hants 9 H2
Benwick Cambs 24 B6
Bere Alston Devon 3 K4
Bere Ferrers Devon 3 K4
Bere Regis Dorset...... 7 L3
Berkeley Gloucs 13 G2
Berkhamsted Herts... 15 G3
Bernisdale Highld 56 D4
Berriedale Highld 65 G5

Berriew Powys 20 F1
Berrow Somset 12 D6
Berwick St John Wilts 13 K8
Berwick-upon-Tweed Nthumb 47 K4
Bethersden Kent 11 G4
Bethesda Gwynd 26 E3
Bettyhill Highld 64 D2
Betws-y-Coed Conwy 27 G4
Betws-yn-Rhos Conwy 27 H3
Beulah Powys 20 D5
Beverley E R Yk 35 G3
Bewdley Worcs 21 L3
Bexhill E Susx 10 F7
Bibury Gloucs 13 L1
Bicester Oxon 14 D2
Bickleigh Devon 5 H6
Biddenden Kent 11 G4
Biddisham Somset 12 E6
Biddulph Staffs 28 F4
Bideford Devon 4 D5
Bidford-on-Avon Warwks 22 C5
Bigbury-on-Sea Devon 3 M6
Biggar S Lans 46 B6
Biggin Hill Gt Lon 10 C3
Biggleswade C Beds 23 M5
Bildeston Suffk 17 H3
Billericay Essex 16 F7
Billingborough Lincs 31 G6
Billingham S on T 38 E2
Billinghay Lincs 31 H4
Billingshurst W Susx 9 K3
Bilsby Lincs 31 K3
Bilsthorpe Notts 30 C4
Binbrook Lincs 35 H7
Binfield Br For 14 F6
Bingham Notts 30 D5
Bingley C Brad 33 K3
Birdlip Gloucs 22 A8
Birkenhead Wirral 32 C7
Birmingham Birm 22 B2
Birstall Leics 30 C8
Birtley Gatesd 43 K6
Bishop Auckland Dur 38 C1
Bishop's Castle Shrops 21 G2
Bishop's Cleeve Gloucs 22 A7
Bishop's Frome Herefs 21 K5
Bishops Lydeard Somset 12 C4
Bishop's Stortford Herts 16 D5
Bishopsteignton Devon 6 C4
Bishopston Swans 19 J7
Bishopstone Swindn 13 M3
Bishop Sutton BaNES 13 G5
Bishop's Waltham Hants 8 F4
Bitchfield Lincs 30 F6
Bitton S Glos 13 G4
Blaby Leics 22 F1
Blackbrook Staffs 28 E6
Blackburn Bl w D 32 F4
Blackford P & K 50 E6
Blackmill Brgnd 19 M7
Blackpool Bpool 32 C3
Black Torrington Devon 4 D6
Blackwater Hants 14 F7
Blackwater IoW 8 F6
Blackwaterfoot N Ayrs 44 C5
Blackwood Caerph 12 C2
Blackwood S Lans 45 L4
Bladon Oxon 14 C3
Blaenau Ffestiniog Gwynd 26 F5
Blaenavon Torfn 12 D1
Blaengarw Brdgnd 19 L6
Blaenporth Cerdgn 18 F2
Blagdon N Som 12 F5
Blair Atholl P & K 54 C7
Blairgowrie P & K 51 G3
Blairmore Ag & B 49 K5
Blakeney Gloucs 13 G1
Blakeney Norfk 23 G6
Blanchland Nthumb 43 G6
Blandford Forum Dorset 7 L2
Blanefield Stirlg 50 B8
Blaxton Donc 34 D6
Blaydon Gatesd 43 J5
Bleadney Somset 12 F4
Bleadon N Som 12 E5
Blean Kent 11 J3
Bleddfa Powys 20 F4

Bletchingley Surrey 10 B3
Bletchley M Keyn 23 J4
Bletsoe Bed 23 K4
Blewbury Oxon 14 C5
Blickling Norfk 25 J3
Blidworth Notts 30 C4
Blindley Heath Surrey 10 C4
Blisland Cnwll 3 G4
Bloxham Oxon 22 E6
Blubberhouses N York 38 B7
Blue Anchor Somset 5 J3
Blyth Nthumb 43 K4
Blyton Lincs 34 E7
Boat of Garten Highld 54 D3
Boddam Abers 61 H5
Bodfari Denbgs 27 J3
Bodfuan Gwynd 26 C6
Bodiam E Susx 10 F5
Bodmin Cnwll 3 G4
Bognor Regis W Susx 9 J6
Bollington Ches E 29 G3
Bolney W Susx 10 B6
Bolsover Derbys 29 L3
Bolton Bolton 32 F6
Bolton Abbey N York 33 J2
Bolton-le-Sands Lancs 37 H6
Bolventor Cnwll 3 H3
Bonar Bridge Highld 64 C8
Bonchester Bridge Border 42 D7
Bo'ness Falk 46 A2
Bonnyrigg Mdloth 46 D4
Bontnewydd Gwynd 26 D4
Bonvilston V Glam 12 B4
Boot Cumb 36 E3
Bootle Cumb 36 E4
Bootle Sefton 32 C7
Bordeaux Guern 6 b1
Boreham Street E Susx 10 E6
Borehamwood Herts 15 J4
Boroughbridge N York 38 D6
Borough Green Kent 10 E3
Borrowash Derbys 29 L6
Borth Cerdgn 20 A2
Borth-y-Gest Gwynd 26 E6
Boscastle Cnwll 3 G2
Bosham W Susx 9 H5
Bosherston Pembks 18 D6
Boston Lincs 31 J5
Boston Spa Leeds 34 B3
Botesdale Suffk 25 H7
Bothel Cumb 41 M7
Bottesford Leics 30 E6
Bottesford N Linc 34 F6
Bough Beech Kent 10 D4
Boughton Street Kent 11 H3
Boulmer Nthumb 47 M7
Bourne Lincs 31 G7
Bourne End Bucks 14 F5
Bournemouth Bmouth 8 B6
Bourton Shrops 21 K2
Bourton-on-the-Water Gloucs 22 C7
Bovey Tracey Devon 6 B4
Bowes Dur 37 M3
Bowmore Ag & B 48 C7
Bowness-on-Solway Cumb 41 M5
Bowness-on-Windermere Cumb 37 G4
Box Wilts 13 J4
Boxford Suffk 17 H4
Bozeat Nhants 23 J4
Bracadale Highld 56 D5
Brackley Nhants 23 G6
Bracknell Br For 14 F6
Bradford C Brad 33 K4
Bradford-on-Avon Wilts 13 J5
Brading IoW 8 F6
Bradwell Derbys 29 J2
Bradwell-on-Sea Essex 17 H6
Bradworthy Devon 4 C4
Brae Shet 61 b4
Braemar Abers 54 E5
Braeswick Ork 65 d2
Braidwood S Lans 45 L3
Brailsford Derbys 29 J5
Braintree Essex 16 F5
Braithwaite Cumb 36 F2
Bramdean Hants 8 F3
Bramfield Suffk 25 K7

Bramham Leeds 34 B3
Bramhope Leeds 33 L3
Bramley Hants 14 D7
Bramley Surrey 9 K2
Brampton Cambs 23 M3
Brampton Cumb 42 D5
Bramshaw Hants 8 D4
Brancaster Norfk 24 E2
Brandesburton E R Yk 35 H3
Brandon Dur 43 J7
Brandon Suffk 24 E6
Brandon Warwks 22 E3
Branscombe Devon 6 E3
Bransgore Hants 8 C6
Branston Lincs 30 F3
Branthwaite Cumb 36 D2
Brassington Derbys 29 J4
Brasted Kent 10 D3
Bratton Wilts 13 J6
Bratton Clovelly Devon 3 K2
Bratton Fleming Devon 4 F4
Braughing Herts 16 C5
Braunton Devon 4 E4
Brayford Devon 4 F4
Breascleit W Isls 62 g3
Breasclete W Isls 62 g3
Brechfa Carmth 19 H4
Brechin Angus 55 J7
Brecon Powys 20 E7
Brede E Susx 11 G6
Bredenbury Herefs 21 K5
Bredhurst Kent 10 F3
Bredon Worcs 22 A6
Bredwardine Herefs 21 G6
Brendon Devon 5 G3
Brent Knoll Somset 12 E6
Brentwood Essex 16 E7
Brenzett Kent 11 H5
Brereton Green Ches E 28 E4
Brewood Staffs 28 F8
Bride IoM 36 C1
Bridestowe Devon 3 L2
Bridge Kent 11 J3
Bridgend Ag & B 48 C6
Bridgend Brdgnd 19 L7
Bridge of Allan Stirlg 50 D6
Bridge of Cally P & K 51 G2
Bridge of Earn P & K 51 G5
Bridge of Orchy Ag & B 53 K6
Bridge of Weir Rens 49 M6
Bridgnorth Shrops 21 L2
Bridgwater Somset 12 D7
Bridlington E R Yk 39 L6
Bridport Dorset 7 H3
Brierfield Lancs 33 H3
Brigg N Linc 35 G6
Brigham Cumb 41 L8
Brighouse Calder 33 K4
Brighstone IoW 8 E7
Brightlingsea Essex 17 J5
Brighton Br & H 10 B7
Brigstock Nhants 23 K2
Brinklow Warwks 22 E3
Brinkworth Wilts 13 K3
Brinyan Ork 65 c3
Bristol Brist 13 G4
Brixham Torbay 6 C6
Brixton Devon 3 L5
Brixton Gt Lon 15 K6
Brixworth Nhants 23 H3
Broad Blunsdon Swindn 13 L3
Broadbridge Heath W Susx 9 L3
Broad Chalke Wilts 13 K8
Broadclyst Devon 6 D3
Broadford Highld 56 F6
Broad Haven Pembks 18 C5
Broadstairs Kent 11 L2
Broadway Worcs 22 C6
Broadwindsor Dorset 7 G2
Brockdish Norfk 25 J7
Brockenhurst Hants 8 D5
Brockford Street Suffk 17 J1
Brockworth Gloucs 21 M8
Brodick N Ayrs 44 D4
Brome Suffk 25 H7
Bromfield Shrops 21 J3
Bromham Bed 23 K5
Bromley Gt Lon 10 C2
Brompton-by-Sawdon N York 39 J5
Brompton Regis Somset 5 H3

Bromsgrove Worcs 22 A3
Bromyard Herefs 21 K5
Bronllys Powys 20 F6
Brooke Norfk 25 K6
Brookland Kent 11 H5
Brookmans Park Herts 15 J4
Broomhill Nthumb 43 K2
Brora Highld 64 F7
Broseley Shrops 21 K1
Brotherton N York 34 B4
Brotton R & Cl 39 G2
Brough Cumb 37 K2
Brough E R Yk 34 F4
Broughton Border 46 B6
Broughton N Linc 34 F6
Broughton-in-Furness Cumb 36 F5
Broughton Moor Cumb 41 K7
Broughton Poggs Oxon 13 M2
Brownhills Wsall 29 H8
Broxburn W Loth 46 B3
Broxted Essex 16 D5
Brundall Norfk 25 K5
Bruton Somset 13 G7
Brynamman Carmth 19 K5
Bryncrug Gwynd 20 A1
Brynmawr Blae G 12 C1
Bubwith E R Yk 34 D3
Buchlyvie Stirlg 50 B7
Buckden Cambs 23 M4
Buckden N York 37 M5
Buckfastleigh Devon 6 B5
Buckhaven Fife 51 H6
Buckhorn Weston Dorset 13 H8
Buckie Moray 60 B3
Buckingham Bucks 23 G6
Buckland Herts 16 C4
Bucklers Hard Hants 8 E5
Buckley Flints 27 L4
Bucklow Hill Ches E 28 E2
Buckminster Leics 30 E7
Bude Cnwll 4 B6
Budleigh Salterton Devon 6 D4
Bugle Cnwll 2 F5
Builth Wells Powys 20 E5
Bulford Wilts 8 C2
Bulkington Warwks 22 E2
Bulphan Thurr 16 E8
Bulwick Nhants 23 K2
Bunessan Ag & B 48 C2
Bungay Suffk 25 K6
Bunny Notts 30 C6
Buntingford Herts 16 C4
Bunwell Norfk 25 H6
Burbage Wilts 13 M5
Bures Essex 17 G4
Burford Oxon 13 M1
Burgess Hill W Susx 10 B6
Burgh by Sands Cumb 42 B6
Burgh Castle Norfk 25 L5
Burghead Moray 59 J3
Burghfield W Berk 14 D6
Burgh le Marsh Lincs 31 K4
Burley Hants 8 C5
Burleydam Ches E 28 D5
Burley in Wharfedale C Brad 33 K3
Burlton Shrops 28 C7
Burneston N York 38 C5
Burnham Market Norfk 24 F2
Burnham-on-Crouch Essex 17 H7
Burnham-on-Sea Somset 12 D6
Burnham Overy Staithe Norfk 24 F2
Burnley Lancs 33 G4
Burnopfield Dur 43 J6
Burntisland Fife 46 C2
Burntwood Staffs 29 H8
Burravoe Shet 61 d3
Burrelton P & K 51 G3
Burrington Devon 4 F5
Burry Port Carmth 19 H6
Burscough Bridge Lancs 32 D5
Bursledon Hants 8 E5
Burton Ches W 27 L3
Burton Agnes E R Yk 39 K6
Burton Bradstock Dorset 7 H3
Burton Fleming E R Yk 39 K6
Burton-in-Kendal Cumb 37 H5
Burton Joyce Notts 30 C5

Burton Latimer
  Nhants 23 J3
Burton upon
  Stather N Linc 34 F5
Burton upon Trent
  Staffs 29 J7
Burwash E Susx 10 E5
Burwell Cambs 16 E1
Burwick Ork 65 c6
Bury Bury 33 G5
Bury St Edmunds
  Suffk 17 G2
Bushey Herts 15 H4
Butley Suffk 17 L3
Buttermere Cumb 36 E2
Butterwick Lincs 31 J5
Buttington Powys 27 K8
Buxted E Susx 10 D6
Buxton Derbys 29 H3
Bwlch Powys 20 F7
Byfleet Surrey 15 H7
Bylchau Conwy 27 H4
Byrness Nthumb 42 F2

C

Cadgwith Cnwll 2 D8
Caerleon Newpt 12 E3
Caernarfon Gwynd 26 D4
Caerphilly Caerph 12 C3
Caersws Powys 20 E2
Caerwent Mons 12 F3
Caerwys Flints 27 J3
Cairndow Ag & B 49 K3
Cairnryan D & G 40 B5
Caister-on-Sea Norfk .. 25 L5
Caistor Lincs 35 H6
Caldbeck Cumb 42 B7
Caldecott Rutlnd 23 J2
Calder Bridge Cumb .. 36 D3
Caldercruix N Lans 45 L2
Caldicot Mons 12 F3
Calfsound Ork 65 d2
Calgary Ag & B 52 B5
Callander Stirlg 50 B6
Callington Cnwll 3 J4
Calne Wilts 13 K4
Calshot Hants 8 E5
Calverton Notts 30 C5
Calvine P & K 54 C7
Camber E Susx 11 H6
Camberley Surrey 14 F7
Cambo Nthumb 43 H4
Camborne Cnwll 2 C6
Cambourne Cambs 16 B2
Cambridge Cambs 16 C2
Cambuslang S Lans 45 K2
Camden Town Gt Lon .. 15 K3
Camelford Cnwll 3 G3
Campbeltown Ag & B .. 44 B5
Candlesby Lincs 31 K3
Cannich Highld 58 C6
Cannington Somset 12 D7
Cannock Staffs 29 G8
Canonbie D & G 42 C4
Canterbury Kent 11 J3
Canvey Island Essex 16 F8
Caoles Ag & B 48 b2
Capel Surrey 9 L2
Capel Bangor Cerdgn .. 20 B3
Capel Curig Conwy 26 F4
Capel St Mary Suffk .. 17 J4
Caputh P & K 50 F3
Carbost Highld 56 D6
Cardiff Cardif 12 C4
Cardigan Cerdgn 18 E2
Cardington Bed 23 L5
Cardross Ag & B 49 L5
Carew Pembks 18 D6
Carfraemill Border 46 F4
Carhampton Somset 5 J3
Cark Cumb 37 G5
Carlabhagh W Isls 62 g3
Carlisle Cumb 42 C6
Carlops Border 46 C4
Carloway W Isls 62 g3
Carlton N York 34 D4
Carlton N York 38 A5
Carlton-on-Trent
  Notts 30 D4
Carluke S Lans 45 L3
Carmarthen Carmth 19 G4
Carnaby E R Yk 39 K6
Carnforth Lancs 37 H6
Carno Powys 20 D2
Carnon Downs Cnwll 2 E6
Carnoustie Angus 51 K4
Carnwath S Lans 46 A3
Carradale Ag & B 44 C4

Carrbridge Highld 59 H6
Carrefour Jersey 7 b1
Carrick Castle Ag & B .. 49 K4
Carronbridge D & G 41 J3
Carrutherstown
  D & G 41 L5
Carsphairn D & G 40 F3
Carstairs S Lans 45 M3
Carterton Oxon 14 A3
Cartmel Cumb 37 G5
Castel Guern. 6 a2
Casterton Cumb 37 J5
Castle Acre Norfk 24 F4
Castlebay W Isls 62 b14
Castle Carrock Cumb .. 42 D6
Castle Cary Somset 13 G7
Castle Donington
  Leics 29 L6
Castle Douglas D & G .. 41 H5
Castleford Wakefd 34 B4
Castlemartin Pembks .. 18 C6
Castle Rising Norfk 24 D4
Castleside Dur 43 H6
Castleton Derbys 29 H2
Castleton N York 39 G3
Castleton Newpt 12 D3
Castletown Highld 65 H2
Castletown IoM 36 b4
Caterham Surrey 10 C3
Catfield Norfk 25 K4
Caton Lancs 37 H6
Catrine E Ayrs 45 J5
Catsfield E Susx 10 F6
Catterick N York 38 C4
Caunton Notts 30 D4
Cawdor Highld 59 G4
Cawsand Cnwll 3 K5
Caxton Cambs 16 B2
Caythorpe Lincs 30 F5
Cayton N York 39 K5
Cemaes IoA 26 C1
Cemmaes Road
  Powys 20 C1
Ceres Fife 51 J5
Cerne Abbas Dorset 7 J2
Cerrigydrudion
  Conwy 27 H5
Chadderton Oldham 33 H6
Chadlington Oxon 14 B2
Chagford Devon 6 A3
Chale IoW 8 E7
Chalfont St Giles
  Bucks 15 G4
Chalfont St Peter
  Bucks 15 G5
Chalford Gloucs 13 J2
Challacombe Devon 4 F3
Challock Kent 11 H3
Chandler's Ford
  Hants 8 E4
Chapel-en-le-Frith
  Derbys 29 H2
Chapel St Leonards
  Lincs 31 L3
Chapeltown Sheff 34 A4
Chapmanslade Wilts .. 13 J6
Chard Somset 6 F2
Charing Kent 11 H4
Charlbury Oxon 14 B2
Charlecote Warwks 22 D5
Charlestown of
  Aberlour Moray ... 59 L5
Charlton Kings
  Gloucs 22 A7
Charlton Marshall
  Dorset 7 L2
Charlwood Surrey 10 B4
Charmouth Dorset 7 G3
Chartham Kent 11 J3
Chatburn Lancs 33 G3
Chatham Medway 10 F2
Chatteris Cambs 24 B7
Chatton Nthumb 47 K6
Chawleigh Devon 4 F6
Chawton Hants 9 J3
Cheadle Staffs 29 G5
Cheadle Stockp 33 H7
Cheddar Somset 12 F6
Cheddleton Staffs 29 G5
Chelford Ches E 28 F3
Chelmsford Essex 16 F6
Cheltenham Gloucs 22 A7
Chepstow Mons 12 F3
Cheriton Hants 8 F3
Cheriton Fitzpaine
  Devon 5 H6
Chertsey Surrey 15 G6
Chesham Bucks 15 G4
Cheshunt Herts 15 K4
Chester Ches W 28 B3
Chesterfield Derbys 29 K3
Chester-le-Street Dur .. 43 K6

Chew Magna BaNES 13 G5
Chewton Mendip
  Somset 13 G6
Chicheley M Keyn 23 J5
Chichester W Susx 9 H5
Chickerell Dorset 7 J4
Chicklade Wilts 13 J7
Chiddingfold Surrey 9 J3
Chieveley W Berk 14 C6
Chigwell Essex 16 C7
Childer Thornton
  Ches W 28 B3
Chillington Devon 6 B7
Chilmark Wilts 13 K7
Chilsworthy Devon 4 C6
Chilton Foliat Wilts 14 A6
Chineham Hants 14 D7
Chinnor Oxon 14 E4
Chippenham Cambs .. 16 E1
Chippenham Wilts 13 J4
Chipperfield Herts 15 G4
Chipping Lancs 32 F3
Chipping Campden
  Gloucs 22 C6
Chipping Norton
  Oxon 22 D7
Chipping Ongar
  Essex 16 D6
Chipping Sodbury
  S Glos 13 H3
Chipping Warden
  Nhants 22 F5
Chirbury Shrops 21 G1
Chirk Wrexhm 27 L6
Chirnside Border 47 J4
Chiseldon Swindn 13 M4
Chitterne Wilts 13 K6
Chittlehamholt
  Devon 4 F5
Chobham Surrey 15 G7
Cholderton Wilts 8 C2
Chorley Lancs 32 E5
Chorleywood Herts .. 15 G4
Christchurch Dorset .. 8 C5
Chudleigh Devon 6 C4
Chudleigh Knighton
  Devon 6 C4
Chulmleigh Devon 4 F6
Churchill Devon 14 A2
Churchstoke Powys .. 21 G2
Church Stretton
  Shrops 21 H2
Churston Ferrers
  Torbay 6 C6
Churt Surrey 9 H3
Cinderford Gloucs 21 K8
Cirencester Gloucs 13 K2
Clachan Ag & B 44 B3
Clachan Highld 56 E5
Clackmannan Clacks .. 50 E7
Clacton-on-Sea Essex .. 17 J5
Clanfield Oxon 14 A4
Claonaig Ag & B 44 C3
Clapham Bed 23 K5
Clapham N York 37 K6
Clare Suffk 16 F3
Clatt Abers 60 C6
Claverdon Warwks 22 C4
Clavering Essex 16 D4
Clawton Devon 4 C7
Clay Cross Derbys 29 K4
Claydon Suffk 17 J4
Cleator Moor Cumb .. 36 D2
Cleethorpes NE Lin .. 35 J6
Cleeve N Som 12 F5
Cleeve Hill Gloucs 22 B7
Cleobury Mortimer
  Shrops 21 K3
Cleobury North
  Shrops 21 K2
Clevedon N Som 12 E4
Cleveleys Lancs 32 C3
Cley next the Sea
  Norfk 25 G2
Cliffe Medway 10 F2
Cliffe N York 34 D4
Cliffe Woods Medway .. 10 F2
Clifton Cumb 37 H2
Clifton upon Teme
  Worcs 21 L4
Climping W Susx 9 K5
Clitheroe Lancs 33 G3
Clola Abers 61 G5
Clophill C Beds 23 K6
Closworth Somset 7 H2
Cloughton N York 39 J4
Clova Angus 55 G6
Clovelly Devon 4 C5
Clovenfords Border 46 E6
Clowne Derbys 30 B3
Clows Top Worcs 21 L3

Clun Shrops 21 G3
Clydach Swans 19 J6
Clydebank W Duns 45 K2
Clynder Ag & B 49 K5
Clynnog-fawr Gwynd .. 26 D5
Clyro Powys 20 F6
Clyst St Mary Devon .. 6 D3
Coalport Wrekin 21 K1
Coalville Leics 29 L7
Coatbridge N Lans 45 K2
Cobham Kent 10 E2
Cockburnspath
  Border 47 H3
Cockermouth Cumb .. 41 L8
Cocking W Susx 9 J4
Coddenham Suffk 17 J2
Codford St Mary
  Wilts 13 K7
Codicote Herts 15 J3
Codnor Derbys 29 L5
Codsall Staffs 21 M1
Coedpoeth Wrexhm .. 27 L5
Coggeshall Essex 17 G5
Colchester Essex 17 H5
Cold Ash W Berk 14 C6
Cold Ashby Nhants 23 G3
Cold Ashton S Glos 13 H4
Coldingham Border 47 J3
Cold Norton Essex 17 G7
Coldstream Border 47 H5
Coleford Gloucs 13 G1
Colerne Wilts 13 J4
Coleshill Warwks 22 C2
Colintraive Ag & B 49 J6
Collier's End Herts 15 K2
Colliston Abers 61 G6
Collingbourne Ducis
  Wilts 13 M6
Collingham Leeds 34 B3
Colmonell S Ayrs 40 C3
Colne Lancs 33 H3
Colne Engaine Essex .. 17 G4
Coln St Aldwyns
  Gloucs 13 L2
Colpy Abers 60 D6
Colsterworth Lincs 30 F7
Coltishall Norfk 25 J4
Colwell Nthumb 43 G4
Colwyn Bay Conwy .. 27 G2
Colyford Devon 6 F3
Colyton Devon 6 F3
Combe Martin Devon .. 4 E3
Compton Surrey 9 J2
Compton W Berk 14 C5
Comrie P & K 50 D5
Congleton Ches E 28 F4
Congresbury N Som .. 12 F5
Coningsby Lincs 31 H4
Conington Cambs 23 M2
Conisbrough Donc 34 C6
Coniston Cumb 36 F4
Connah's Quay Flints .. 27 L3
Connel Ag & B 52 F7
Conon Bridge Highld .. 58 E4
Consett Dur 43 H6
Constantine Cnwll 2 D7
Contin Highld 58 D4
Conwy Conwy 27 G3
Cookham W & M 14 F5
Coolham W Susx 9 L4
Coombe Bissett Wilts .. 8 B3
Coombe Hill Gloucs .. 21 M7
Copdock Suffk 17 J3
Copford Green Essex .. 17 G5
Copley Dur 38 B2
Copplestone Devon .. 5 G6
Copthorne W Susx 10 B4
Corbière Jersey 7 a2
Corbridge Nthumb 43 G5
Corby Nhants 23 J2
Corby Glen Lincs 30 F7
Corfe Somset 6 F1
Corfe Castle Dorset 7 M4
Corgarff Abers 55 G4
Cornhill-on-Tweed
  Nthumb 47 H5
Cornwood Devon 3 L5
Corpach Highld 53 H3
Corrie N Ayrs 44 D4
Corris Gwynd 26 F8
Corsham Wilts 13 J4
Corston Wilts 13 J3
Corton Suffk 25 M6
Corwen Denbgs 27 H4
Coryton Thurr 16 F8
Cosby Leics 22 F2
Cotebrook Ches W 28 D4
Cotherstone Dur 38 A2
Cottenham Cambs 16 C1
Cottered Herts 15 B4
Cottingham E R Yk 35 G4
Coulport Ag & B 49 K5

Coulter S Lans 46 B6
Countesthorpe Leics 23 G2
Coupar Angus P & K 51 G3
Cove Highld 62 D8
Coventry Covtry 22 E3
Coverack Cnwll 2 D8
Cowbit Lincs 31 H7
Cowbridge V Glam 12 B4
Cowden Kent 10 D4
Cowdenbeath Fife 51 G7
Cowes IoW 8 E6
Cowfold W Susx 9 L4
Cowling N York 33 J3
Coxheath Kent 10 F3
Coxwold N York 38 E5
Coylton S Ayrs 45 H6
Coylumbridge Highld .. 54 D3
Crackington Haven
   Cnwll 4 B7
Cracoe N York 37 M7
Crafthole Cnwll 3 J5
Craigellachie Moray 59 L5
Craighouse Ag & B 48 D6
Craignure Ag & B 52 E6
Craigrothie Fife 51 J5
Crail Fife 51 L6
Crailing Border 47 G7
Cramlington Nthumb ... 43 K4
Cranborne Dorset 8 B4
Cranbrook Kent 10 F5
Cranfield C Beds 23 K6
Cranham Gloucs 21 M8
Cranleigh Surrey 9 K2
Crarae Ag & B 49 H4
Craster Nthumb 47 M7
Crathie Abers 54 F5
Crathorne N York 38 E3
Craven Arms Shrops 21 H3
Crawford S Lans 46 A7
Crawfordjohn S Lans ... 45 M5
Crawley W Susx 10 B5
Crawley Down
   W Susx 10 B4
Creag Ghoraidh
   W Isls 62 c10
Creagorry W Isls 62 c10
Credenhill Herefs 21 H6
Crediton Devon 5 G7
Creetown D & G 40 F6
Cregneash IoM 36 a4
Cressage Shrops 21 K1
Crewe Ches E 28 E4
Crewkerne Somset 7 G2
Crianlarich Stirlg 53 K7
Criccieth Gwynd 26 D6
Crickhowell Powys 20 F7
Cricklade Wilts 13 L3
Crieff P & K 50 D5
Crimond Abers 61 H4
Crinan Ag & B 49 G4
Cringleford Norfk 25 J5
Cromarty Highld 59 G3
Cromdale Highld 59 J4
Cromer Norfk 25 J2
Cromford Derbys 29 K4
Cromwell Notts 30 E4
Crook Dur 43 J7
Crooklands Cumb 37 H5
Cropredy Oxon 22 F5
Cropton N York 39 G4
Crosby IoM 36 b3
Crosby Sefton 32 C6
Crossford Fife 46 B2
Crossford S Lans 45 L3
Cross Hands Carmth 19 H5
Crosshill S Ayrs 45 G6
Cross in Hand E Susx ... 10 D6
Crosskeys Caerph 12 D3
Crossmichael D & G 41 H5
Crossway Green
   Worcs 21 M4
Crosthwaite Cumb 37 G4
Crowborough E Susx 10 D5
Crowcombe Somset 5 K4
Crowhurst E Susx 10 F6
Crowland Lincs 31 H8
Crowle N Linc 34 E5
Crowthorne Wokham ... 14 F7
Croxton Kerrial Leics .. 30 K6
Croy Highld 59 G4
Croyde Devon 4 D4
Croydon Gt Lon 15 K7
Cruden Bay Abers 61 H5
Crudgington Wrekin 28 D7
Crudwell Wilts 13 K3
Crynant Neath 19 K5
Cuckfield W Susx 10 B5
Cuckney Notts 30 C3

Cuddington Ches W 28 D3
Cudworth Barns 34 B6
Cuffley Herts 15 K4
Culgaith Cumb 37 J1
Cullen Moray 60 C3
Cullompton Devon 5 J6
Culmstock Devon 5 K6
Cumbernauld N Lans ... 45 L1
Cuminestown Abers 60 E4
Cummertrees D & G 41 L5
Cumnock E Ayrs 45 J5
Cumnor Oxon 14 C4
Cumrew Cumb 42 D6
Cupar Fife 51 J5
Currie C Edin 46 C3
Curry Rivel Somset 12 B8
Cwmbran Torfn 12 D2
Cwmystwyth Cerdgn ... 20 C3
Cymer Neath 19 L6
Cynwyl Elfed Carmth ... 19 G4

D

Dailly S Ayrs 40 D2
Dairsie Fife 51 J5
Dalbeattie D & G 41 J5
Dalby IoM 36 a3
Dale Pembks 18 B5
Dalgety Bay Fife 46 C2
Dalhalvaig Highld 64 E3
Dalkeith Mdloth 46 D3
Dallas Moray 59 J4
Dalmally Ag & B 53 J7
Dalmellington E Ayrs .. 45 H7
Dalry N Ayrs 45 G3
Dalrymple E Ayrs 45 G6
Dalston Cumb 42 B6
Dalton D & G 41 L4
Dalton-in-Furness
   Cumb 36 F6
Dalwhinnie Highld 54 A5
Damerham Hants 8 B4
Danbury Essex 16 F6
Darlington Darltn 38 C2
Darras Hall Nthumb 43 J3
Darrington Wakefd 34 B5
Dartford Kent 10 D2
Dartington Devon 6 B5
Dartmouth Devon 6 C6
Darvel E Ayrs 45 J4
Darwen Bl w D 32 F5
Datchet W & M 15 G6
Dava Highld 59 H5
Davenham Ches W 28 D3
Daventry Nhants 23 G4
Daviot Highld 58 F5
Dawlish Devon 6 C4
Deal Kent 11 L3
Dearham Cumb 41 L7
Debenham Suffk 17 J2
Deddington Oxon 22 F6
Dedham Essex 17 H4
Deeping St James
   Lincs 31 H8
Deeping St Nicholas
   Lincs 31 H7
Deganwy Conwy 27 G2
Delabole Cnwll 3 G3
Denbigh Denbgs 27 J3
Denby Dale Kirk 33 L6
Denham Bucks 15 G5
Denholm Border 46 F7
Denmead Hants 9 G5
Dennington Suffk 17 K1
Denny Falk 50 D8
Densole Kent 11 K4
Dent Cumb 37 K5
Denton Tamesd 33 H7
Derby C Derb 29 K6
Derbyhaven IoM 36 b4
Dereham Norfk 25 G4
Dersingham Norfk 24 E3
Dervaig Ag & B 52 B5
Desborough Nhants 23 H3
Desford Leics 22 F1
Devil's Bridge Cerdgn .. 20 B3
Devizes Wilts 13 K5
Dewsbury Kirk 33 L5
Didcot Oxon 14 C5
Didmarton Gloucs 13 J3
Digby Lincs 31 G4
Dilwyn Herefs 21 H5
Dinas-Mawddwy
   Gwynd 27 G7
Dingwall Highld 58 E4
Dinnington Rothm 30 B2
Dippen Ag & B 44 C4
Diseworth Leics 29 L7
Dishforth N York 38 D6
Disley Ches E 29 G2

Diss Norfk 25 H7
Ditchling E Susx 10 B6
Dittisham Devon 6 C6
Ditton Priors Shrops ... 21 K2
Dobwalls Cnwll 3 H4
Docking Norfk 24 E3
Doddington Cambs 24 B6
Doddington Kent 11 G3
Doddington
   Nthumb 47 K6
Dodworth Barns 33 L6
Dolgellau Gwynd 26 F7
Dollar Clacks 50 E6
Dolphinton S Lans 46 B5
Dolton Devon 4 E6
Dolwyddelan Conwy 26 F5
Doncaster Donc 34 C6
Donington Lincs 31 H6
Dorchester Dorset 7 K3
Dorchester-on-
   Thames Oxon 14 D4
Dordon Warwks 22 D1
Dores Highld 58 E5
Dorking Surrey 9 L2
Dornie Highld 57 H6
Dornoch Highld 59 G1
Dorrington Shrops 21 J1
Dorstone Herefs 21 G6
Douglas IoM 36 c3
Douglas S Lans 45 L5
Dounby Ork 65 b3
Doune Stirlg 50 C6
Dousland Devon 3 L4
Dover Kent 11 L4
Doveridge Derbys 29 H6
Dowally P & K 50 E3
Downderry Cnwll 3 J5
Downham Market
   Norfk 24 D5
Downton Wilts 8 C4
Drakes Broughton
   Worcs 22 A5
Draycott Somset 12 F6
Drayton Norfk 25 J4
Drayton Oxon 14 C4
Driffield E R Yk 39 J7
Drimnin Highld 52 C5
Droitwich Spa Worcs ... 22 A4
Dronfield Derbys 29 K3
Droxford Hants 8 F4
Drumbeg Highld 63 G4
Drummore D & G 40 C7
Drumnadrochit
   Highld 58 D6
Drymen Stirlg 50 A7
Drynoch Highld 56 D6
Duddington Nhants 23 K1
Dudley Dudley 22 A2
Duffield Derbys 29 K5
Dufftown Moray 59 L5
Duffus Moray 59 K3
Dulnain Bridge
   Highld 59 H6
Dulverton Somset 5 H4
Dumbarton W Duns 49 M5
Dumfries D & G 41 K4
Dunbar E Loth 47 G2
Dunbeath Highld 65 H5
Dunblane Stirlg 50 D6
Dunchurch Warwks 22 F3
Dundee C Dund 51 H4
Dundonald S Ayrs 45 G4
Dundonnell Highld 57 K1
Dundrennan D & G 41 H6
Dunfermline Fife 50 B2
Dunkeld P & K 50 F3
Dunlop E Ayrs 45 H3
Dunnet Highld 65 H2
Dunning P & K 50 E5
Dunoon Ag & B 49 K5
Dunragit D & G 40 C6
Duns Border 47 H4
Dunscore D & G 41 J4
Dunsfold Surrey 9 K3
Dunsford Devon 6 B3
Dunsop Bridge
   Lancs 32 F2
Dunstable C Beds 15 G2
Dunster Somset 5 H3
Duntish Dorset 7 K2
Dunure S Ayrs 44 F6
Dunvant Swans 19 J6
Dunvegan Highld 56 C4
Dunwich Suffk 25 L3
Durham Dur 43 J7
Durness Highld 63 J2
Duror Highld 53 G5
Durrington Wilts 8 C2
Durris Abers 55 L5
Dursley Gloucs 13 H3
Duxford Cambs 16 D3
Dyce C Aber 55 M3

Dyffryn Ardudwy
   Gwynd 26 E7
Dymchurch Kent 11 J5
Dymock Gloucs 21 K7

E

Eaglesfield D & G 42 A4
Eaglesham E Rens 45 J3
Ealing Gt Lon 15 J5
Earby Lancs 33 H3
Eardisley Herefs 21 G5
Earith Cambs 24 B7
Earley Wokham 14 E6
Earls Barton Nhants ... 23 J4
Earls Colne Essex 17 G4
Earl Shilton Leics 22 F1
Earlston Border 46 F6
Earsham Norfk 25 K6
Easdale Ag & B 48 F2
Easebourne W Susx 9 J4
Easington Dur 43 L7
Easington E R Yk 35 K5
Easingwold N York 38 E6
East Ayton N York 39 J5
East Barkwith Lincs 31 H2
East Bergholt Suffk 17 J4
Eastbourne E Susx 10 E7
East Chinnock
   Somset 7 H1
Eastchurch Kent 11 H2
East Cowes IoW 8 E6
East Dean E Susx 10 D8
East Dean W Susx 9 J4
East Goscote Leics 30 C7
East Grinstead
   W Susx 10 C4
East Harling Norfk 25 G6
East Hoathly E Susx 10 D6
East Horsley Surrey 15 H8
East Ilsley W Berk 14 C5
East Kilbride S Lans ... 45 J3
East Lavant W Susx 9 H5
Eastleigh Hants 8 E4
East Linton E Loth 46 F3
East Lulworth Dorset 7 L4
Easton Suffk 17 K2
East Prawle Devon 6 B7
East Preston W Susx 9 K5
Eastriggs D & G 42 A5
East Rudham Norfk 24 F3
Eastry Kent 11 L3
East Saltoun E Loth 46 E3
East Stoke Notts 30 D5
East Tilbury Thurr 10 E1
East Wittering
   W Susx 9 H6
East Witton N York 38 B5
Eastwood Notts 29 L5
Eaton Socon Cambs 23 L4
Ebbw Vale Blae G 12 C1
Ebchester Dur 43 H6
Ecclefechan D & G 41 M4
Eccles Border 47 H5
Eccleshall Staffs 28 F6
Echt Abers 55 K4
Eckington Derbys 29 L2
Eckington Worcs 22 A6
Edderton Highld 58 F2
Eddleston Border 46 C5
Edenbridge Kent 10 C4
Edinbane Highld 56 D4
Edinburgh C Edin 46 C3
Edington Wilts 31 H3
Edmundbyers Dur 43 H6
Ednam Border 47 G6
Edwinstowe Notts 30 C3
Edzell Angus 55 J7
Effingham Surrey 15 H7
Eggesford Devon 4 F6
Eggleston Dur 37 M2
Egham Surrey 15 G6
Eglingham Nthumb 47 K7
Eglwyswrw Pembks 18 E3
Egremont Cumb 36 D3
Egton Bridge N York ... 39 H3
Elan Village Powys 20 D4
Elgin Moray 59 K3
Elgol Highld 56 E7
Elham Kent 11 J4
Elie Fife 51 K6
Elkesley Notts 30 D3
Elkstone Gloucs 13 K1
Elland Calder 33 K5
Ellesmere Shrops 28 B6
Ellesmere Port
   Ches W 28 B3
Ellingham Norfk 25 K6
Ellon Abers 61 G6

Elloughton E R Yk 34 F4
Elmstead Market
  Essex................17 H5
Elsdon Nthumb.........43 G3
Elsrickle S Lans......46 B5
Elstead Surrey.........9 J2
Elstree Herts.........15 J4
Elterwater Cumb......37 G3
Eltisley Cambs........16 B2
Elton Cambs...........23 L2
Elveden Suffk.........24 F7
Elvetham Heath Hants..14 E7
Elvington C York......34 D3
Elworthy Somset........5 J4
Ely Cambs.............24 C7
Embleton Nthumb.......47 M7
Embo Highld...........64 E8
Empingham Rutlnd......30 F8
Emsworth Hants.........9 H5
Enderby Leics.........22 F1
Enfield Gt Lon........15 K4
Ennerdale Bridge
  Cumb................36 D2
Enstone Oxon..........14 B2
Epping Essex..........16 C6
Epsom Surrey..........15 J7
Epworth N Linc........34 E6
Errogie Highld........58 E6
Errol P & K...........51 H4
Erwood Powys..........20 E6
Esher Surrey..........15 H7
Eskdale Green Cumb....36 E4
Eskdalemuir D & G.....42 A3
Essendine Rutlnd......31 G8
Essendon Herts........15 J3
Eston R & Cl..........38 E2
Etal Nthumb...........47 J6
Etchingham E Susx.....10 F5
Eton W & M............15 G6
Ettington Warwks......22 D5
Ettrick Border........46 D7
Ettrickbridge Border..46 E7
Evanton Highld........58 E3
Evercreech Somset.....13 G7
Eversley Hants........14 E7
Evesham Worcs.........22 B6
Ewen Gloucs...........13 K2
Ewhurst Surrey.........9 K2
Ewyas Harold Herefs...21 H7
Exebridge Somset.......5 H5
Exeter Devon...........6 C3
Exford Somset..........5 H4
Exminster Devon........6 C3
Exmouth Devon..........6 D4
Eye C Pete............23 M1
Eye Suffk.............25 H7
Eyemouth Border.......47 J4
Eynsford Kent.........10 D2
Eynsham Oxon..........14 B3

F

Failsworth Oldham.....33 H6
Fairbourne Gwynd......26 E8
Fairford Gloucs.......13 L2
Fairlie N Ayrs........44 F3
Fairlight E Susx......11 G6
Fakenham Norfk........24 F3
Fala Mdloth...........46 E4
Faldingworth Lincs....31 G2
Falfield S Glos.......13 G3
Falkirk Falk..........50 E8
Falkland Fife.........51 H6
Falmouth Cnwll.........2 E7
Falstone Nthumb.......42 E3
Fareham Hants..........8 F5
Faringdon Oxon........14 A4
Farnborough Hants.....14 F7
Farnell Angus.........51 L2
Farnham Surrey.........9 H2
Farnham Common
  Bucks...............15 G5
Farningham Kent.......10 D2
Far Sawrey Cumb.......37 G4
Fauldhouse W Loth.....45 M2
Faversham Kent........11 H3
Fawley Hants...........8 E5
Fazeley Staffs........22 C1
Fearnan P & K.........50 C3
Felixstowe Suffk......17 K4
Felsted Essex.........16 E5
Felton Nthumb.........43 J2
Feltwell Norfk........24 E6
Fenny Bentley
  Derbys..............29 J5
Fenny Bridges Devon...6 E3
Fenny Compton
  Warwks.............22 E5
Fenny Drayton Leics...22 E1
Fenwick E Ayrs........45 H4

Ferndown Dorset........8 B5
Fernhill Heath Worcs..21 M4
Fernhurst W Susx.......9 J3
Fernilee Derbys.......29 G3
Ferring W Susx.........9 J5
Ferryhill Dur.........43 K8
Fettercairn Abers.....55 K6
Ffestiniog Gwynd......26 F5
Filby Norfk...........25 L4
Filey N York..........39 K5
Fincham Norfk.........24 E5
Finchingfield Essex...16 E4
Findhorn Moray........59 J3
Findochty Moray.......60 C3
Findon W Susx..........9 L5
Finedon Nhants........23 J3
Finningham Suffk......17 H1
Finningley Donc.......34 D6
Finstown Ork..........65 b4
Fintry Stirlg.........50 C7
Fionnphort Ag & B.....48 C2
Firle E Susx..........10 D7
Fishbourne IoW.........8 F6
Fishguard Pembks......18 C3
Fittleworth W Susx.....9 J5
Fitzhead Somset........5 K8
Five Oaks Jersey.......7 c2
Fladdabister Shet.....61 c6
Flamborough E R Yk....39 L6
Flamstead Herts.......15 H4
Fleet Hants...........14 F7
Fleetwood Lancs.......32 C3
Flimby Cumb...........41 K7
Flint Flints..........27 K3
Flitwick C Beds.......23 K6
Flixton N York........39 K5
Flore Nhants..........23 G4
Fochabers Moray.......59 L4
Folkestone Kent.......11 K5
Folkingham Lincs......31 G6
Fontmell Magna
  Dorset..............7 L1
Fontwell W Susx........9 J5
Ford Nthumb...........47 J6
Fordcombe Kent........10 D4
Fordingbridge Hants....8 C4
Fordoun Abers.........55 K6
Fordwich Kent.........11 J3
Forest Guern...........6 a2
Forest Row E Susx.....10 C5
Forfar Angus..........51 J2
Formby Sefton.........32 C6
Forres Moray..........59 J4
Fort Augustus Highld..58 C7
Forteviot P & K.......50 F5
Forth S Lans..........45 M3
Fortingall P & K......50 C3
Forton Lancs..........32 E2
Fortrose Highld.......58 F4
Fortuneswell Dorset....7 J6
Fort William Highld...53 H4
Foston Lincs..........30 E5
Four Crosses Powys....27 L7
Four Marks Hants.......9 G5
Fowey Cnwll............3 G5
Fownhope Herefs.......21 J6
Foxdale IoM...........36 b3
Foyers Highld.........58 D7
Framlingham Suffk.....17 K2
Frampton Dorset.......7 J3
Frant E Susx..........10 E5
Fraserburgh Abers.....61 G3
Freckenham Suffk......24 D8
Freckleton Lancs......32 D4
Frensham Surrey........9 H2
Freshwater IoW.........8 D6
Fressingfield Suffk...25 J7
Freswick Highld.......65 J2
Fridaythorpe E R Yk...39 H7
Frilford Oxon.........14 B4
Frinton-on-Sea Essex..17 K5
Friockheim Angus......51 K2
Fritton Norfk.........25 L5
Frizington Cumb.......36 D2
Frocester Gloucs......13 H2
Frodsham Ches W.......28 C3
Frome Somset..........13 H6
Froxfield Wilts.......14 A6
Funtington W Susx......9 H5
Furnace Ag & B........49 J4
Furness Vale Derbys...29 G2
Fyfield Essex.........16 D6
Fyfield Oxon..........14 B4
Fyvie Abers...........60 E5

G

Gailey Staffs.........28 F8
Gainford Dur..........38 B2
Gainsborough Lincs....34 E7

Gairloch Highld.......57 H2
Gairlochy Highld......53 J3
Galashiels Border.....46 E6
Galgate Lancs.........37 H7
Galston E Ayrs........45 H4
Gamlingay Cambs.......16 B3
Gamston Notts.........30 D3
Ganllwyd Gwynd........26 F7
Garboldisham Norfk....25 G7
Gardenstown Abers.....60 E3
Garelochhead Ag & B...49 K4
Garforth Leeds........34 B4
Gargrave N York.......33 H2
Garlieston D & G......40 F6
Garlogie Abers........55 L4
Garrigill Cumb........42 E7
Garstang Lancs........32 E3
Garth Powys...........20 D5
Garvald E Loth........46 F3
Garve Highld..........58 C3
Gatehouse of Fleet
  D & G...............41 G6
Gateshead Gatesd......43 K5
Gaydon Warwks.........22 E5
Gayton Norfk..........24 E4
Gedney Drove End
  Lincs...............31 K6
Gedney Hill Lincs.....31 J8
Georgeham Devon........4 D4
Gerrards Cross Bucks..15 G5
Gifford E Loth........46 F3
Giggleswick N York....37 L6
Gillingham Dorset.....13 H8
Gillingham Medway.....10 F2
Gillingham Norfk......25 L6
Gilling West N York...38 B3
Gills Highld..........65 J1
Gilmerton P & K.......50 E4
Gilsland Nthumb.......42 E5
Gilwern Mons..........21 G8
Girton Cambs..........16 C2
Girvan S Ayrs.........40 C3
Gisburn Lancs.........33 G2
Glamis Angus..........51 J3
Glanton Nthumb........47 K7
Glapwell Derbys.......30 B3
Glasbury Powys........20 F6
Glasgow C Glas........45 J2
Glaston Rutlnd........23 J1
Glastonbury Somset....12 F7
Glemsford Suffk.......17 G3
Glenbarr Ag & B.......44 A4
Glenborrodale Highld..52 D5
Glencaple D & G.......41 K5
Glencoe Highld........53 H5
Glendaruel Ag & B.....49 H5
Glendevon P & K.......50 E6
Glenelg Highld........57 H7
Glenfarg P & K........51 G5
Glenfinnan Highld.....52 F3
Glenkindie Abers......55 H3
Glenlivet Moray.......59 K6
Glenluce D & G........40 C6
Glen Maye IoM.........36 b3
Glenridding Cumb......37 G2
Glenrothes Fife.......51 H6
Glentham Lincs........35 G7
Glossop Derbys........33 J7
Gloucester Gloucs.....21 M7
Glyn Ceiriog Wrexhm...27 K6
Glyncorrwg Neath......19 L5
Glynde E Susx.........10 C7
Glynneath Neath.......19 L5
Glyntawe Powys........20 C8
Gnosall Staffs........28 F7
Goathland N York......39 H3
Goathurst Somset......12 D7
Gobowen Shrops........27 L6
Godalming Surrey.......9 J2
Godmanchester
  Cambs...............23 M4
Godshill IoW...........8 F7
Godstone Surrey.......10 C3
Goginan Cerdgn........20 B3
Golborne Wigan........32 F6
Goldhanger Essex......17 G6
Golspie Highld........64 D4
Gomshall Surrey.......9 K2
Goodwick Pembks.......18 C3
Goole E R Yk..........34 E4
Goostrey Ches E.......28 E3
Gordon Border.........47 G5
Gorebridge Mdloth.....46 D4
Gorey Jersey..........7 c1
Goring Oxon...........14 D5
Gorleston on Sea
  Norfk...............25 L5
Gorran Haven Cnwll.....2 F6
Gorseinon Swans.......19 J6
Gosberton Lincs.......31 H6
Gosforth Cumb.........36 D3
Gosforth N u Ty.......43 J5

Gosport Hants..........8 F5
Goudhurst Kent........10 F4
Gourock Inver.........49 K5
Gowerton Swans........19 J6
Goxhill N Linc........35 H5
Grain Medway..........11 G2
Grainthorpe Lincs.....35 K6
Grampound Cnwll........2 F6
Grandes Rocques
  Guern...............6 a1
Grange Cumb...........36 F2
Grangemouth Falk......50 E8
Grange-over-Sands
  Cumb................37 G5
Grantham Lincs........30 F6
Grantown-on-Spey
  Highld..............59 J6
Grantshouse Border....47 H4
Grasmere Cumb.........37 G3
Grassington N York....38 A6
Graveley Herts........16 B4
Gravesend Kent........10 E2
Grays Thurr...........10 E1
Great Ayton N York....38 F3
Great Badminton
  S Glos..............13 H3
Great Bardfield Essex.16 E4
Great Barford Bed.....23 L5
Great Bircham Norfk...24 E3
Great Blakenham
  Suffk...............17 J3
Great Casterton
  Rutlnd..............30 F8
Great Chesterford
  Essex...............16 D3
Great Dalby Leics.....30 D7
Great Dunmow
  Essex...............16 E5
Great Durnford Wilts...8 B3
Great Gidding Cambs...23 L3
Great Gransden
  Cambs...............16 B2
Greatham Hants.........9 H3
Great Harwood
  Lancs...............33 G4
Great Haywood
  Staffs..............29 G7
Great Hockham
  Norfk...............25 G6
Great Kimble Bucks....14 F3
Great Langdale
  Cumb................36 F3
Great Malvern Worcs...21 L5
Great Massingham
  Norfk...............24 E4
Great Missenden
  Bucks...............14 F4
Great Notley Essex....16 F5
Great Ponton Lincs....30 F6
Great Sampford
  Essex...............16 E4
Great Saughall
  Ches W..............28 B3
Great Shefford
  W Berk..............14 B6
Great Shelford
  Cambs...............16 C3
Great Smeaton
  N York..............38 D3
Greatstone-on-Sea
  Kent................11 J6
Great Tew Oxon........22 E7
Great Torrington
  Devon...............4 E5
Great Wakering
  Essex...............17 G8
Great Waltham
  Essex...............16 E6
Great Witley Worcs....21 L4
Great Yarmouth
  Norfk...............25 L5
Great Yeldham Essex...16 F4
Greenfield Flints.....27 K3
Green Hammerton
  N York..............38 E7
Greenhead Nthumb......42 E5
Greenhow Hill N York..38 B6
Greenlaw Border.......47 G5
Greenloaning P & K....50 D6
Greenock Inver........49 L5
Greenodd Cumb.........36 F5
Greetham Rutlnd.......30 F8
Gresford Wrexhm.......27 L4
Greta Bridge Dur......38 B3
Gretna D & G..........42 B5
Gretna Green D & G....42 B5
Greystoke Cumb........42 C8
Grimsby NE Lin........35 J5
Grimsthorpe Lincs.....31 G7
Grindleford Derbys....29 J3
Gringley on the Hill
  Notts...............34 E7

Groby Leics 30 B8
Grosmont Mons 21 H7
Grouville Jersey 7 c2
Grove Oxon 14 B5
Guardbridge Fife 51 J5
Guestling Green
  E Susx 11 G6
Guildford Surrey 9 K2
Guisborough R & Cl 38 F2
Guiseley Leeds 33 K3
Guist Norfk 25 G4
Gullane E Loth 46 E2
Gunness N Linc 34 E5
Gunnislake Cnwll 3 K4
Gunthorpe Notts 30 D5
Gurnard IoW 8 E6
Gussage All Saints
  Dorset 8 A5
Gutcher Shet 61 d2
Guyhirn Cambs 24 B5
Gweek Cnwll 2 D7
Gwernymynydd
  Flints 27 K4
Gwithian Cnwll 2 C6
Gwyddelwern
  Denbgs 27 J5

H

Hackland Ork 65 b3
Hackness N York 39 J4
Hackney Gt Lon 15 K5
Haddenham Bucks 14 E3
Haddenham Cambs 24 C7
Haddington E Loth 46 F3
Haddiscoe Norfk 25 L6
Hadleigh Essex 16 F8
Hadleigh Suffk 17 H3
Hadlow Kent 10 E4
Hagworthingham
  Lincs 31 J3
Hailsham E Susx 10 E7
Halberton Devon 5 J6
Hales Norfk 25 K6
Halesowen Dudley 22 A3
Halesworth Suffk 25 K7
Halifax Calder 33 K4
Halkirk Highld 65 G2
Halstead Essex 16 F4
Halstead Kent 10 D3
Haltwhistle Nthumb 42 E5
Halwell Devon 6 B6
Halwill Junction
  Devon 4 D7
Hambledon Hants 9 G4
Hamble-le-Rice
  Hants 8 E5
Hambleton Lancs 32 D3
Hamilton S Lans 45 K3
Hammersmith Gt Lon ... 15 J6
Hampsthwaite
  N York 38 C7
Hamstead Kent 11 H5
Handcross W Susx 10 B5
Handley Ches W 28 C4
Hanley C Stke 28 F5
Happisburgh Norfk 25 K3
Harbertonford
  Devon 6 B6
Hardwicke Gloucs 13 H1
Hare Street Herts 16 C4
Harewood Leeds 33 L3
Harewood End
  Herefs 21 J7
Harlech Gwynd 26 E6
Harleston Norfk 25 J7
Harlosh Highld 56 C5
Harlow Essex 16 C6
Harlyn Cnwll 2 E4
Haroldswick Shet 61 d1
Harpenden Herts 15 H3
Harrogate N York 38 C7
Harrold Bed 23 K5
Harrow Gt Lon 15 H5
Harston Cambs 16 C3
Hartburn Nthumb 43 H3
Hartest Suffk 17 G3
Hartfield E Susx 10 D5
Hartington Derbys 29 H4
Hartland Devon 4 C5
Hartlepool Hartpl 43 M8
Hartley Wintney
  Hants 14 E7
Hartpury Gloucs 21 L7
Harvington Worcs 22 B5
Harwich Essex 17 K4
Haseley Warwks 22 D4
Haslemere Surrey 9 J3

Hassocks W Susx 10 B6
Hastings E Susx 10 F7
Hatch Beauchamp
  Somset 12 D8
Hatfield Donc 34 D5
Hatfield Herts 15 J3
Hatfield Broad Oak
  Essex 16 D5
Hatfield Heath Essex ... 16 D5
Hatfield Peverel
  Essex 16 F6
Hatherleigh Devon 4 E6
Hathern Leics 30 B7
Hathersage Derbys 29 J2
Hatton Abers 61 H5
Havant Hants 9 G5
Havenstreet IoW 8 F6
Haverfordwest
  Pembks 18 C5
Haverhill Suffk 16 E3
Hawarden Flints 27 L3
Hawes N York 37 L4
Hawick Border 46 F7
Hawkedon Suffk 16 F3
Hawkhurst Kent 10 F5
Hawkinge Kent 11 K4
Hawkshead Cumb 37 G4
Hawnby N York 38 E4
Haworth C Brad 33 J3
Haxby C York 38 F7
Haxey N Linc 34 E6
Haydon Bridge
  Nthumb 42 F5
Hayle Cnwll 2 C6
Hay-on-Wye Powys 21 G6
Haywards Heath
  W Susx 10 B6
Hazel Grove Stockp 28 F2
Heacham Norfk 24 D3
Headcorn Kent 11 G4
Heanor Derbys 29 L5
Heath Derbys 29 L3
Heathfield E Susx 10 E6
Hebden Bridge
  Calder 33 J4
Heckington Lincs 31 G5
Hedge End Hants 8 E4
Hednesford Staffs 29 G8
Hedon E R Yk 35 J6
Helensburgh Ag & B 49 L5
Hellifield N York 37 L7
Helmingham Suffk 17 K2
Helmsdale Highld 65 G6
Helmsley N York 38 F5
Helpringham Lincs 31 G5
Helsby Ches W 28 C3
Helston Cnwll 2 C7
Hemel Hempstead
  Herts 15 H3
Hempnall Norfk 25 J6
Hemsby Norfk 25 L4
Hemsworth Wakefd 34 B5
Hemyock Devon 5 K6
Hendy Carmth 19 J6
Henfield W Susx 9 L4
Henham Essex 16 D4
Henley-in-Arden
  Warwks 22 C4
Henley-on-Thames
  Oxon 14 E5
Henllan Denbgs 27 J3
Henlow C Beds 23 L6
Henstead Suffk 25 L7
Henstridge Somset 7 K1
Hereford Herefs 21 J6
Hermitage W Berk 14 C6
Herne Bay Kent 11 J2
Hersden Kent 11 K3
Herstmonceux
  E Susx 10 E6
Hertford Herts 15 K3
Hessle E R Yk 35 G4
Heswall Wirral 27 L2
Hethersett Norfk 25 H5
Heversham Cumb 37 H5
Hexham Nthumb 43 G5
Hexworthy Devon 3 M4
Heybrook Bay Devon 3 K6
Heysham Lancs 37 G7
Heytesbury Wilts 13 J6
Hibaldstow N Linc 35 G6
Hickstead W Susx 10 B6
Higham Ferrers
  Nhants 23 K4
Highampton Devon 4 E6
High Bentham
  N York 37 J6
Highbridge Somset 12 D6
Highclere Hants 14 B7
High Ercall Wrekin 28 D7
Higher Town IoS 2 b1
High Halden Kent 11 G5

High Hesket Cumb 42 C7
Highley Shrops 21 L3
High Roding Essex 16 E5
Highworth Swindn 13 M3
High Wycombe
  Bucks 14 F4
Hildenborough Kent 10 D4
Hill Brow Hants 9 H4
Hill of Fearn Highld 59 G2
Hillswick Shet 61 b3
Hilmarton Wilts 13 K4
Hilton Derbys 29 J6
Hinckley Leics 22 E2
Hinderwell N York 39 G2
Hindhead Surrey 9 J3
Hindon Wilts 13 J7
Hingham Norfk 25 G5
Hipswell N York 38 B4
Hirwaun Rhondd 12 A2
Histon Cambs 16 C2
Hitcham Suffk 17 H3
Hitchin Herts 23 M7
Hockley Essex 17 G7
Hockliffe C Beds 23 K7
Hoddesdon Herts 15 K3
Hodnet Shrops 28 D6
Hogsthorpe Lincs 31 L3
Holbeach Lincs 31 J7
Holbeton Devon 3 L5
Holbrook Suffk 17 J4
Holbury Hants 8 E5
Holkham Norfk 24 F2
Hollingbourne Kent 11 G3
Holmbury St Mary
  Surrey 9 L2
Holmes Chapel
  Ches E 28 E3
Holme upon
  Spalding Moor
  E R Yk 34 E3
Holmfirth Kirk 33 K6
Holmrook Cumb 36 D4
Holne Devon 6 A5
Holsworthy Devon 4 C6
Holt Norfk 25 H3
Holt Wilts 13 J5
Holt Wrexhm 28 B4
Holt Heath Worcs 21 L4
Holton le Clay Lincs ... 35 J6
Holyhead IoA 26 B2
Holy Island Nthumb 47 L5
Holytown N Lans 45 L2
Holywell Dorset 7 J2
Holywell Flints 27 K3
Homersfield Suffk 25 J7
Honingham Norfk 25 H5
Honington Suffk 24 F7
Honiton Devon 6 E2
Hook Hants 14 E7
Hoo St Werburgh
  Medway 10 F2
Hoolam E Susx 29 J2
Hope Derbys 29 J2
Hope Devon 6 A7
Hope Flints 27 L4
Hope Bowdler
  Shrops 21 J2
Hopeman Moray 59 K3
Hope under
  Dinmore Herefs 21 J5
Hopton on Sea
  Norfk 25 M5
Horam E Susx 10 D6
Horley Surrey 10 B4
Hornby Lancs 37 J6
Horncastle Lincs 31 H3
Horndean Hants 9 G4
Horns Cross Devon 4 D5
Hornsea E R Yk 35 H3
Horrabridge Devon 3 L4
Horsey Norfk 25 L4
Horsforth Leeds 33 L3
Horsham W Susx 9 L3
Horsley Nthumb 43 H5
Horton Dorset 8 B5
Horton Somset 6 F1
Horton-cum-Studley
  Oxon 14 D3
Horton-in-
  Ribblesdale
  N York 37 L6
Horwich Bolton 32 F5
Hoton Leics 30 C7
Houghton-le-Spring
  Sundld 43 K6
Houghton on the
  Hill Leics 23 G1
Hounslow Gt Lon 15 H6
Houton Ork 65 b4
Hove Br & H 10 B7
Hovingham N York 38 F5
Howden E R Yk 34 E4
Hoxne Suffk 25 J7

Hoylake Wirral 32 B7
Hoyland Nether
  Barns 34 B6
Hucknall Notts 30 B5
Huddersfield Kirk 33 K5
Hugh Town IoS 2 a2
Hull, Kingston upon
  C KuH 35 G4
Humberston NE Lin 35 J6
Humbie E Loth 46 E4
Hume Border 47 G5
Hungerford W Berk 14 B6
Hunmanby N York 39 K5
Hunstanton Norfk 24 D2
Huntingdon Cambs 23 M3
Huntley Gloucs 21 L7
Huntly Abers 60 C5
Hursley Hants 8 E4
Hurstbourne Priors
  Hants 8 E2
Hurstbourne Tarrant
  Hants 14 B7
Hurst Green E Susx 10 F5
Hurst Green Lancs 32 F3
Hurstpierpoint
  W Susx 10 B6
Hurworth-on-Tees
  Darltn 38 C3
Husbands Bosworth
  Leics 23 G2
Husborne Crawley
  C Beds 23 K6
Huttoft Lincs 31 L3
Hutton-le-Hole
  N York 39 G4
Hyde Tamesd 33 H7
Hynish Ag & B 48 b3
Hythe Hants 8 E5
Hythe Kent 11 J5

I

Ibstock Leics 29 K8
Ideford Devon 6 C4
Ilchester Somset 12 F8
Ilfracombe Devon 4 E3
Ilkeston Derbys 29 L5
Ilkley C Brad 33 K3
Ilminster Somset 7 G1
Immingham NE Lin 35 H5
Immingham Dock
  NE Lin 35 H5
Inchnadamph Highld ... 65 H5
Ingatestone Essex 16 E7
Ingham Lincs 30 F2
Ingleton N York 37 K6
Ingoldmells Lincs 31 L3
Inkberrow Worcs 22 B5
Innellan Ag & B 49 K6
Innerleithen Border 46 D3
Insch Abers 60 D6
Insh Highld 54 C4
Instow Devon 4 D4
Inveralloch Abers 61 G3
Inveran Highld 64 C7
Inveraray Ag & B 49 J3
Inverasdale Highld 57 H2
Inverbervie Abers 55 L6
Invergarry Highld 53 K2
Invergordon Highld 58 F3
Invergowrie P & K 51 H4
Inverinate Highld 53 J6
Inverkeilor Angus 51 L2
Inverkeithing Fife 46 B2
Inverkeithny Abers 60 D5
Inverkip Inver 49 K6
Invermoriston
  Highld 58 D7
Inverness Highld 58 F5
Inverurie Abers 55 L3
Ipplepen Devon 6 B5
Ipstones Staffs 29 G5
Ipswich Suffk 17 J3
Irchester Nhants 23 J4
Ireby Cumb 42 A7
Ironbridge Wrekin 21 K1
Irthlingborough
  Nhants 23 K3
Irvine N Ayrs 45 G4
Isle of Whithorn D & G . 40 F7
Isleornsay Highld 57 G7
Islington Gt Lon 15 K5
Itchen Abbas Hants 8 F3
Iver Bucks 15 G5
Ivinghoe Bucks 15 G3
Ivybridge Devon 3 M5
Iwade Kent 11 G2
Iwerne Minster
  Dorset 7 L1
Ixworth Suffk 25 G8

J

Jarrow S Tyne 43 K5
Jedburgh Border 47 G7
Jerbourg Guern 6 b2
Jevington E Susx 10 D7
John o' Groats Highld .. 65 J1
Johnshaven Abers 55 L7
Johnston Pembks 18 C5
Johnstone Rens 49 M6
Jurby IoM 36 c1

K

Kames Ag & B 49 H6
Keelby Lincs 35 H5
Kegworth Leics 30 B6
Keighley C Brad 33 J3
Keiss Highld 65 J2
Keith Moray 60 B4
Keld N York 37 L3
Kelham Notts 30 D4
Kelso Border 47 G6
Kelvedon Essex 17 G5
Kemble Gloucs 13 K2
Kemnay Abers 55 K3
Kempsey Worcs 21 M5
Kempston Bed 23 K5
Kendal Cumb 37 H4
Kenilworth Warwks 22 D3
Kenmore P & K 50 D3
Kennacraig Ag & B 49 G6
Kennford Devon 6 C3
Kenninghall Norfk 25 G7
Kentallen Highld 53 G5
Kentford Suffk 16 F2
Kenton Devon 6 C4
Kerry Powys 20 F2
Kessingland Suffk 25 L6
Keswick Cumb 36 F2
Kettering Nhants 23 J3
Kettlewell N York 37 M6
Ketton Rutlnd 23 K1
Keymer W Susx 10 B6
Keynsham BaNES 13 G4
Keyston Cambs 23 K3
Keyworth Notts 30 C6
Kibworth
    Beauchamp Leics ...23 G2
Kidderminster
    Worcs 21 M3
Kidlington Oxon 14 C3
Kidsgrove Staffs 28 F4
Kidwelly Carmth 19 G5
Kielder Nthumb 42 D3
Kilberry Ag & B 48 F6
Kilbirnie N Ayrs 45 G3
Kilburn Derbys 29 K5
Kilburn N York 38 E5
Kilchattan Ag & B 44 E3
Kilchoan Highld 52 C4
Kilchrenan Ag & B 49 J2
Kilcreggan Ag & B 49 K5
Kildale N York 38 F3
Kildrummy Abers 55 H3
Kildwick N York 33 J3
Kilfinan Ag & B 49 H5
Kilgetty Pembks 18 E5
Kilham E R Yk 39 K6
Kilkenzie Ag & B 44 B5
Kilkhampton Cnwll 4 C6
Killearn Stirlg 50 B7
Killiecrankie P & K 54 D7
Killin Stirlg 50 B4
Kilmacolm Inver 49 L6
Kilmany Fife 51 J5
Kilmarnock E Ayrs 45 H4
Kilmartin Ag & B 49 G4
Kilmaurs E Ayrs 45 H4
Kilmelford Ag & B 49 G3
Kilmorack Highld 58 D5
Kilninver Ag & B 49 G2
Kilsyth N Lans 50 C8
Kilve Somset 5 K3
Kilwinning N Ayrs 45 G4
Kimberley Norfk 25 H5
Kimbolton Cambs 23 L4
Kinbrace Highld 64 E5
Kincardine Fife 50 E7
Kincardine O'Neil
    Abers 55 J4
Kincraig Highld 54 C4
Kineton Warwks 22 E5
Kingsbarns Fife 51 K5
Kingsbridge Devon 6 B7
Kingsbury Warwks 22 D2
Kingsclere Hants 14 C7
King's Cliffe Nhants 23 K1
Kingsdown Kent 11 L4

Kingsfold W Susx 9 L3
Kingskerswell Devon 6 C5
Kingsland Herefs 21 H4
Kings Langley Herts 15 H4
Kingsley Staffs 29 G5
King's Lynn Norfk 24 D4
King's Mills Guern 6 a2
Kingsnorth Kent 11 H4
King's Somborne
    Hants 8 D3
King's Stag Dorset 7 K2
King's Stanley Gloucs .. 13 H2
Kingsteignton
    Devon 6 C4
Kingstone Herefs 21 H6
Kingston on Spey
    Moray 59 L3
Kingston upon Hull
    C KuH 35 G4
Kingston upon
    Thames Gt Lon 15 J6
Kingswear Devon 6 C6
Kings Worthy Hants 8 E3
Kington Herefs 21 G5
Kingussie Highld 54 B4
Kinlochbervie
    Highld 63 H3
Kinlocheil Highld 53 G3
Kinlochewe Highld 57 J3
Kinlochleven Highld 53 J5
Kinloch Rannoch
    P & K 50 C2
Kinloss Moray 59 J3
Kinmel Bay Conwy 27 H2
Kinneff Abers 55 L6
Kinross P & K 50 F6
Kintbury W Berk 14 B6
Kintore Abers 55 L3
Kippen Stirlg 50 C7
Kirby Misperton
    N York 39 G5
Kirby Muxloe Leics 22 F1
Kirkabister Shet 61 c6
Kirkbean D & G 41 K6
Kirkbride Cumb 42 A6
Kirkburton Kirk 33 K5
Kirkby Knows 32 D6
Kirkby-in-Ashfield
    Notts 30 B4
Kirkby Lonsdale
    Cumb 37 J5
Kirkby Malzeard
    N York 38 C5
Kirkbymoorside
    N York 39 G5
Kirkby Stephen
    Cumb 37 K3
Kirkcaldy Fife 51 H7
Kirkcolm D & G 40 B5
Kirkconnel D & G 45 K6
Kirkcowan D & G 40 D5
Kirkcudbright
    D & G 41 G6
Kirkham Lancs 32 D4
Kirkhill Highld 58 E5
Kirkinner D & G 40 E6
Kirkintilloch E Duns 45 K1
Kirk Langley
    Derbys 29 K6
Kirk Michael IoM 36 b2
Kirkmichael P & K 50 F2
Kirkmichael S Ayrs 45 G6
Kirknewton
    Nthumb 47 J6
Kirkoswald Cumb 42 D7
Kirkoswald S Ayrs 44 F6
Kirkpatrick-Fleming
    D & G 42 B5
Kirkwall Ork 65 c4
Kirkwhelpington
    Nthumb 43 H4
Kirriemuir Angus 51 J2
Kirton Lincs 31 J6
Kirton in Lindsey
    N Linc 34 F6
Kislingbury Nhants 23 H4
Knaphill Surrey 15 G7
Knaresborough
    N York 38 D7
Knarsdale Nthumb 42 E6
Knebworth Herts 15 J2
Knighton Powys 21 G3
Knightwick Worcs 21 L5
Knockan Highld 63 H6
Knockin Shrops 27 L7
Knottingley Wakefd 34 C4
Knowl Hill W & M 14 F5
Knutsford Ches E 28 E3
Kyleakin Highld 57 G6
Kyle of Lochalsh
    Highld 57 G6
Kylerhea Highld 57 G7

L

Laceby NE Lin 35 H6
Ladock Cnwll 2 E5
Ladybank Fife 51 H5
Laggan Highld 54 A5
La Grève de Lecq
    Jersey 7 a1
Laide Highld 62 E8
Lairg Highld 64 C6
Lakenheath Suffk 24 E7
Lamberhurst Kent 10 E5
Lambourn W Berk 14 B6
Lamerton Devon 3 K3
Lamington S Lans 46 A6
Lamlash N Ayrs 44 D5
Lampeter Cerdgn 19 J2
Lamport Nhants 23 H3
Lanark S Lans 45 M4
Lancaster Lancs 37 H6
Lanchester Dur 43 J6
Lancing W Susx 9 L5
L'Ancresse Guern 6 b1
Landrake Cnwll 3 J5
Langham Rutlnd 30 E8
Langholm D & G 42 B4
Langport Somset 12 E8
Langthwaite N York 38 A3
Langtoft E R Yk 39 J6
Langton Matravers
    Dorset 8 A7
Langwathby Cumb 42 D7
Langworth Lincs 31 G3
Lanivet Cnwll 3 G4
Lapford Devon 5 G6
Largoward Fife 51 J6
Largs N Ayrs 44 F2
Larkhall S Lans 45 L3
Larkhill Wilts 8 B2
Lastingham N York 39 G4
Latchingdon Essex 17 G7
Latheron Highld 65 H4
Lauder Border 46 F5
Laugharne Carmth 18 F5
Launceston Cnwll 3 J3
Laurencekirk Abers 55 K6
Laurieston D & G 41 G5
Lavenham Suffk 17 H3
Lawers P & K 50 C3
Laxey IoM 36 c3
Laxfield Suffk 25 K8
Lazonby Cumb 42 D7
Leadenham Lincs 30 F5
Leaden Roding Essex ... 16 E6
Leadgate Dur 43 J6
Leadhills S Lans 45 M6
Leamington Spa
    Warwks 22 D4
Leatherhead Surrey 15 J7
Lechlade on Thames
    Gloucs 13 M2
Ledbury Herefs 21 L6
Lee Devon 4 E3
Leebotwood Shrops 21 J1
Leeds Leeds 33 L4
Leek Staffs 29 G4
Leeming Bar N York 38 C4
Lee-on-the-Solent
    Hants 8 F5
Legbourne Lincs 31 J2
Leicester C Leic 23 G1
Leigh Kent 10 D4
Leigh Wigan 32 F6
Leigh Sinton Worcs 21 L5
Leighton Buzzard
    C Beds 23 J7
Leintwardine Herefs 21 H3
Leiston Suffk 17 M2
Lelant Cnwll 2 C6
Lendalfoot S Ayrs 40 C3
Lenham Kent 11 G3
Lennoxtown E Duns 50 B8
Leominster Herefs 21 J4
L'Erée Guern 6 a2
Lerwick Shet 61 c6
Leslie Abers 55 J3
Leslie Fife 51 H6
Lesmahagow S Lans 45 L4
Leswalt D & G 40 B5
L'Etacq Jersey 7 a1
Letchworth Garden
    City Herts 16 B4
Letham Angus 51 K3
Letterston Pembks 18 C4
Leuchars Fife 51 J5
Leven E R Yk 35 H3
Leven Fife 51 J6
Levens Cumb 37 H4
Leverburgh W Isls 62 e7
Lewes E Susx 10 C7
Lewisham Gt Lon 10 C2

Leyburn N York 38 B4
Leyland Lancs 32 E5
Leysdown-on-Sea
    Kent 11 H2
Lhanbryde Moray 59 L3
Libberton S Lans 46 A5
Lichfield Staffs 29 H8
Lidgate Suffk 16 F2
Lifton Devon 3 J3
Lightwater Surrey 15 G7
Lilliesleaf Border 46 F7
Limpley Stoke Wilts 13 H5
Lincoln Lincs 30 F3
Lindale Cumb 37 G5
Lingfield Surrey 10 C4
Linlithgow W Loth 46 A3
Linton Cambs 16 D3
Linton Kent 10 F4
Liphook Hants 9 H3
Liskeard Cnwll 3 H4
Liss Hants 9 H3
Lissington Lincs 31 G2
Litcham Norfk 24 F4
Litchfield Hants 14 C7
Little Abington
    Cambs 16 D3
Little Berkhamsted
    Herts 15 K3
Littleborough Rochdl ... 33 H5
Little Brickhill M Keyn .. 23 J6
Little Bytham Lincs 30 F7
Little Clacton Essex 17 J5
Little Gaddesden
    Herts 15 G3
Littlehampton
    W Susx 9 K5
Littleport Cambs 24 D6
Littlestone-on-Sea
    Kent 11 J3
Little Stretton Shrops ... 21 H2
Little Torrington
    Devon 4 E5
Little Walsingham
    Norfk 25 G3
Liverpool Lpool 32 C7
Livingston W Loth 46 B3
Lizard Cnwll 2 D8
Llanaelhaearn
    Gwynd 26 C5
Llanarmon Dyffryn
    Ceiriog Wrexhm 27 K6
Llanarthne Carmth 19 H4
Llanbedr Gwynd 26 E6
Llanbedr-Dyffryn-
    Clwyd Denbgs 27 K4
Llanbedrog Gwynd 26 C6
Llanberis Gwynd 26 E4
Llanbister Powys 20 F3
Llanbrynmair Powys 20 D1
Llandarog Carmth 19 H5
Llandderfel Gwynd 27 H6
Llanddulas Conwy 27 H3
Llandeilo Carmth 19 J4
Llandinam Powys 20 E2
Llandissilio Pembks 18 E4
Llandovery Carmth 19 K3
Llandre Cerdgn 20 B2
Llandrillo Denbgs 27 J6
Llandrindod Wells
    Powys 20 E4
Llandrinio Powys 27 L7
Llandudno Conwy 27 G2
Llandwrog Gwynd 26 D4
Llandybie Carmth 19 J5
Llandysul Cerdgn 19 G3
Llanelli Carmth 19 H6
Llanerchymedd IoA 26 D2
Llanerfyl Powys 27 J8
Llanfachraeth IoA 26 C2
Llanfair Caereinion
    Powys 27 J8
Llanfair Dyffryn
    Clwyd Denbgs 27 J4
Llanfairfechan
    Conwy 26 F3
Llanfairpwllgwyngyll
    IoA 26 D3
Llanfair Talhaiarn
    Conwy 27 H3
Llanfair Waterdine
    Shrops 21 G3
Llanfarian Cerdgn 20 A3
Llanfyllin Powys 27 K7
Llangadfan Powys 27 H8
Llangadog Carmth 19 K4
Llangammarch Wells
    Powys 20 D5
Llangedwyn Powys 27 K7
Llangefni IoA 26 D3
Llangeinor Brdgnd 19 L7
Llangeler Carmth 19 G3
Llangennith Swans 19 G6

Llangernyw Conwy 27 G3
Llangoed IoA 26 E2
Llangollen Denbgs 27 K5
Llangors Powys 20 F7
Llangrannog Cerdgn .. 18 F2
Llangurig Powys 20 D3
Llangynidr Powys 20 F7
Llangynog Powys 27 J7
Llanhamlach Powys .. 20 E7
Llanharan Rhondd 12 B3
Llanidloes Powys 20 D2
Llanilar Cerdgn 20 B3
Llanllechid Gwynd 26 E3
Llannefydd Conwy 27 H3
Llanrhaeadr-ym-
  Mochnant Powys 27 J7
Llanrhidian Swans 19 H6
Llanrhystud Cerdgn .. 20 A4
Llanrug Gwynd 26 E4
Llanrwst Conwy 27 G4
Llansanffraid Glan
  Conwy Conwy 27 G3
Llansannan Conwy 27 H3
Llansantffraid
  Cerdgn 19 H1
Llansantffraid-ym-
  Mechain Powys 27 K7
Llansawel Carmth 19 J3
Llansteffan Carmth 19 G5
Llanthony Mons 21 G7
Llantrisant Rhondd .. 12 B3
Llantwit Major
  V Glam 5 J1
Llanuwchllyn Gwynd .. 27 G6
Llanvetherine Mons .. 21 H8
Llanvihangel
  Crucorney Mons ... 21 G7
Llanwddyn Powys 27 J7
Llanwnda Gwynd 26 D4
Llanwnen Carmth 19 K3
Llanwrtyd Wells
  Powys 20 D5
Llanybydder Carmth .. 19 H2
Llanymynech Powys .. 27 L7
Llanystumdwy
  Gwynd 26 D6
Llay Wrexhm 27 L4
Llechryd Cerdgn 18 F3
Llwyngwril Gwynd 26 E8
Llwynmawr Wrexhm .. 27 K6
Llynclys Shrops 27 L7
Llyswen Powys 20 F6
Lochailort Highld 52 E3
Lochaline Highld 52 D6
Locharbriggs D & G .. 41 K4
Lochawe Ag & B 53 H7
Loch Baghasdail
  W Isls 62 c12
Lochboisdale W Isls ... 62 c12
Lochbuie Ag & B 52 D7
Lochcarron Highld 57 H5
Lochdonhead Ag & B .. 52 E7
Lochearnhead Stirlg .. 50 B4
Lochgair Ag & B 49 H4
Lochgilphead Ag & B .. 49 G4
Lochgoilhead Ag & B .. 49 K3
Lochinver Highld 63 G5
Lochmaben D & G 41 L4
Lochmaddy W Isls 62 d8
Loch nam Madadh
  W Isls 62 d8
Lochranza N Ayrs 44 D3
Lochwinnoch Rens 45 G2
Lockerbie D & G 41 L4
Lockton N York 39 H4
Loddon Norfk 25 K6
Lofthouse N York 38 B6
Loftus R & Cl 39 G2
London Gt Lon 15 K5
London Colney Herts .. 15 J4
Long Ashton N Som ... 12 F4
Long Bennington
  Lincs 30 E5
Long Buckby Nhants .. 23 G4
Longburton Dorset 7 J1
Long Compton
  Warwks 22 D6
Long Crendon Bucks .. 14 E3
Long Eaton Derbys 30 B6
Longford Gloucs 21 M7
Longformacus
  Border 47 G4
Longframlington
  Nthumb 43 J2
Longham Dorset 8 B6
Longhorsley Nthumb .. 43 J3
Longhoughton
  Nthumb 47 M7
Long Itchington
  Warwks 22 E4
Long Lawford
  Warwks 22 F3

Long Marston N York .. 34 C2
Long Melford Suffk 17 G3
Longniddry E Loth 46 E3
Longnor Shrops 21 J1
Longnor Staffs 29 H4
Long Preston N York .. 37 L7
Longridge Lancs 32 F3
Longridge W Loth 45 M2
Longside Abers 61 G5
Long Stratton Norfk .. 25 J6
Long Sutton Lincs 31 K7
Long Sutton Somset .. 12 F8
Longton Lancs 32 D4
Longtown Cumb 42 B5
Longville in the Dale
  Shrops 21 J2
Looe Cnwll 3 H5
Lossiemouth Moray ... 59 K3
Lostwithiel Cnwll 3 G5
Loughborough Leics .. 30 B7
Louth Lincs 31 J2
Lowdham Notts 30 D5
Lower Diabaig Highld .. 57 H4
Lower Dicker E Susx .. 10 D6
Lower Peover Ches E .. 28 E3
Lower Swell Gloucs ... 22 C7
Lowestoft Suffk 25 M6
Loweswater Cumb 36 E2
Lowick Nhants 23 K3
Lowick Nthumb 47 K5
Low Row N York 37 M4
Lubenham Leics 23 H2
Ludborough Lincs 35 J7
Ludgershall Wilts 8 D2
Ludham Norfk 25 K4
Ludlow Shrops 21 J3
Lugton E Ayrs 45 H3
Lugwardine Herefs 21 J6
Lumphanan Abers 55 J4
Lumsden Abers 55 H3
Lunan Angus 51 L2
Lupton Cumb 37 H5
Luss Ag & B 49 L4
Lusta Highld 56 C4
Luton Luton 15 H2
Lutterworth Leics 22 F2
Lybster Highld 65 H4
Lydbury North
  Shrops 21 J2
Lydd Kent 11 H6
Lydford Devon 3 L3
Lydford on Fosse
  Somset 12 F7
Lydham Shrops 21 G2
Lydney Gloucs 13 G2
Lyme Regis Dorset 7 G3
Lyminge Kent 11 J4
Lymington Hants 8 D6
Lymm Warrtn 28 E2
Lympne Kent 11 J5
Lyndhurst Hants 8 D5
Lyneham Wilts 13 K4
Lyness Ork 65 b5
Lyng Somset 12 E7
Lynmouth Devon 5 G3
Lynton Devon 4 F3
Lyonshall Herefs 21 G5
Lytham St Anne's
  Lancs 32 C4
Lythe N York 39 H3

M

Mablethorpe Lincs 31 K2
Macclesfield Ches E .. 28 F3
Macduff Abers 60 E3
Machrihanish Ag & B .. 44 A5
Machynlleth Powys 20 C1
Macmerry E Loth 46 E3
Maentwrog Gwynd 26 F5
Maerdy Rhondd 12 B2
Maesteg Brdgnd 19 L7
Maghull Sefton 32 D6
Maiden Bradley Wilts .. 13 H7
Maidencombe Torbay .. 6 C6
Maidenhead W & M 14 F5
Maiden Newton
  Dorset 7 J3
Maidstone Kent 10 F3
Mainsriddle D & G 41 K6
Malborough Devon 6 A7
Maldon Essex 17 G6
Malham N York 37 L6
Mallaig Highld 52 D2
Mallwyd Gwynd 27 G8
Malmesbury Wilts 13 J3
Malpas Ches W 28 C5
Maltby Rothm 34 C7
Malton N York 39 G6
Malvern Worcs 21 L5

Malvern Wells Worcs .. 21 L6
Manaccan Cnwll 2 D7
Manchester Manch 33 G6
Manea Cambs 24 C6
Manningtree Essex 17 J4
Manorbier Pembks 18 D6
Mansfield Notts 30 B4
Marazanvose Cnwll 2 E5
Marazion Cnwll 2 B7
March Cambs 24 B6
Marchwiel Wrexhm 28 B5
Marden Kent 10 F4
Mareham le Fen
  Lincs 31 J4
Margaretting Essex ... 16 E6
Margate Kent 11 L2
Mark Somset 12 E6
Mark Cross E Susx 10 E5
Market Bosworth
  Leics 22 E1
Market Deeping
  Lincs 31 G8
Market Drayton
  Shrops 28 D6
Market Harborough
  Leics 23 H2
Market Lavington
  Wilts 13 K6
Market Rasen Lincs ... 35 H7
Market Warsop
  Notts 30 C3
Market Weighton
  E R Yk 34 F3
Markfield Leics 30 B8
Markham Moor
  Notts 30 D3
Marksbury BaNES 13 G5
Marks Tey Essex 17 G5
Marlborough Wilts 13 M4
Marloes Pembks 18 B5
Marlow Bucks 14 F5
Marnhull Dorset 7 K3
Marshfield S Glos 13 H4
Marsh Gibbon Bucks .. 14 D2
Marske-by-the-Sea
  R & Cl 38 F2
Martin Lincs 31 G4
Martinstown Dorset ... 7 J3
Martlesham Heath
  Suffk 17 K3
Martock Somset 7 H1
Marton Warwks 22 E4
Marykirk Abers 55 K7
Maryport Cumb 41 K7
Mary Tavy Devon 3 L3
Marywell Abers 55 J5
Masham N York 38 C5
Matfield Kent 10 E4
Matlock Derbys 29 K4
Mattingley Hants 14 E7
Mauchline E Ayrs 45 H5
Maud Abers 60 F4
Maughold IoM 36 d2
Maulden C Beds 23 K6
Mawgan Porth Cnwll ... 2 E4
Mawnan Smith Cnwll .. 2 D7
Maybole S Ayrs 45 G6
Mayfield E Susx 10 E5
Mayfield Staffs 29 H5
Meare Somset 12 F6
Measham Leics 29 K8
Medstead Hants 9 G3
Meeth Devon 5 G2
Meifod Powys 27 K8
Meigle P & K 51 H3
Melbourn Cambs 16 C3
Melbourne Derbys 29 K7
Meliden Denbgs 27 J2
Melksham Wilts 13 J5
Melling Lancs 37 J6
Melmerby Cumb 42 B7
Melrose Border 46 F6
Meltham Kirk 33 K5
Melton Constable
  Norfk 25 H3
Melton Mowbray
  Leics 30 D7
Melvaig Highld 57 G2
Melvich Highld 64 E2
Memsie Abers 61 G3
Memus Angus 51 H2
Menai Bridge IoA 26 E3
Mentmore Bucks 14 F3
Meopham Kent 10 E2
Mere Wilts 7 H7
Meriden Solhll 22 D3
Merthyr Tydfil Myr Td .. 12 B2
Merton Devon 4 E6
Messingham N Linc ... 34 F6
Metfield Suffk 25 K7
Methil Fife 51 J6
Methlick Abers 60 F5

Methven P & K 50 F4
Methwold Norfk 24 E6
Mevagissey Cnwll 2 F6
Mexborough Donc 34 B6
Miabhig W Isls 62 f3
Miavaig W Isls 62 f3
Micheldever Hants 8 F2
Mickleton Dur 37 M2
Mickleton Gloucs 22 C6
Midbea Ork 65 c2
Middleham N York 38 B4
Middle Rasen Lincs ... 35 G7
Middlesbrough
  Middsb 38 E2
Middleton Cheney
  Nhants 22 F6
Middleton-in-
  Teesdale Dur 37 M2
Middleton-on-Sea
  W Susx 9 J5
Middleton on the
  Wolds E R Yk 34 F2
Middleton Stoney
  Oxon 14 C2
Middle Town IoS 2 a2
Middle Wallop Hants .. 8 D3
Middlewich Ches E 28 E3
Middlezoy Somset 12 E7
Midhurst W Susx 9 J4
Midsomer Norton
  BaNES 13 G6
Mid Yell Shet 61 d2
Milborne Port
  Somset 7 J1
Mildenhall Suffk 24 E7
Milfield Nthumb 47 J6
Milford Surrey 9 J2
Milford Haven
  Pembks 18 C5
Milford on Sea Hants .. 8 D6
Millbrook Cnwll 3 K5
Millbrook Jersey 7 b2
Millom Cumb 36 E5
Millport N Ayrs 44 F3
Milnathort P & K 50 F6
Milngavie E Duns 45 J1
Milton Abbas Dorset ... 7 K2
Milton Abbot Devon 3 K3
Milton Damerel
  Devon 4 D6
Milton Ernest Bed 23 K5
Milton Keynes
  M Keyn 23 J6
Milverton Somset 5 K5
Minchinhampton
  Gloucs 13 J2
Minehead Somset 5 J3
Minster Kent 11 H2
Minster Kent 11 L2
Minsterley Shrops 28 B8
Minster Lovell Oxon ... 14 A3
Mintlaw Abers 61 G4
Mirfield Kirk 33 K5
Misterton Notts 34 E7
Misterton Somset 7 H2
Mitcheldean Gloucs ... 21 K7
Mobberley Ches E 28 E2
Mochrum D & G 40 E6
Modbury Devon 3 M5
Moffat D & G 41 L2
Mold Flints 27 K4
Moniaive D & G 41 H3
Monifieth Angus 51 K4
Monkleigh Devon 4 D5
Monkton S Ayrs 45 G5
Monmouth Mons 21 J8
Montacute Somset 7 H1
Montford Bridge
  Shrops 28 B7
Montgomery Powys 28 F1
Montrose Angus 51 L2
Mont Saint Guern 6 a2
Monyash Derbys 29 H3
Monymusk Abers 55 K3
Morchard Bishop
  Devon 5 G6
Morcott Rutlnd 23 J1
Mordiford Herefs 21 J6
Morebattle Border 47 H7
Morecambe Lancs 37 G6
Moreton Dorset 7 K3
Moretonhampstead
  Devon 6 B3
Moreton-in-Marsh
  Gloucs 22 C6
Morfa Nefyn Gwynd ... 26 B5
Morley Leeds 33 L4
Morpeth Nthumb 43 J3
Morston Norfk 25 G2
Mortehoe Devon 4 D3
Mortimer W Berk 14 D7
Morville Shrops 21 K2

Morwenstow Cnwll 4 B5
Mossat Abers 55 H3
Mosstodloch Moray ... 59 L4
Mosterton Dorset 7 H2
Mostyn Flints 27 K2
Motherby Cumb 37 G1
Motherwell N Lans 45 K3
Moulsford Oxon 14 D5
Moulton Nhants 23 H4
Mountain Ash
  Rhondd 12 B2
Mountsorrel Leics 30 C2
Mousehole Cnwll 2 B7
Moy Highld 58 F5
Muchalls Abers 55 M5
Much Birch Herefs 21 J7
Much Hadham Herts .. 16 C5
Much Marcle Herefs 21 K6
Much Wenlock
  Shrops 21 K1
Muddiford Devon 4 E4
Muirdrum Angus 51 K3
Muirhead Angus 51 H4
Muirkirk E Ayrs 45 K5
Muir of Ord Highld ... 58 D4
Muker N York 37 L4
Mullion Cnwll 2 D8
Mundesley Norfk 25 K3
Mundford Norfk 24 E6
Mungrisdale Cumb 42 B8
Munlochy Highld 58 E4
Munslow Shrops 21 J2
Musselburgh E Loth ... 46 D3
Muthill P & K 50 D5

N

Nacton Suffk 17 K4
Nailsea N Som 12 F4
Nailsworth Gloucs 13 J2
Nairn Highld 59 G4
Nantgaredig Carmth .. 19 H4
Nantwich Ches E 28 D5
Narberth Pembks 18 E5
Narborough Norfk 24 E4
Naseby Nhants 23 G3
Navenby Lincs 30 F4
Nayland Suffk 17 H4
Nazeing Essex 16 C6
Neath Neath 19 K6
Necton Norfk 24 F5
Needham Market
  Suffk 17 J2
Nefyn Gwynd 26 C5
Nelson Lancs 33 H3
Nesscliffe Shrops 28 B7
Neston Ches W 27 L3
Nether Stowey
  Somset 12 C7
Nether Wasdale Cumb . 36 E6
Nethy Bridge Highld ... 54 D3
Nettlebed Oxon 14 B5
Nettleham Lincs 30 F3
Nevern Pembks 18 E3
New Abbey D & G 41 K5
New Aberdour Abers ... 60 F3
New Alresford Hants 8 F3
Newark-on-Trent
  Notts 30 E4
Newarthill N Lans 45 L2
Newbiggin Dur 37 L1
Newbiggin N York 38 A5
Newbiggin-by-the-
  Sea Nthumb 43 K3
Newbigging S Lans ... 46 A5
Newbold on Stour
  Warwks 22 D5
New Bolingbroke
  Lincs 31 J4
Newborough IoA 26 D4
Newbridge Caerph 12 C2
Newbridge D & G 41 K4
Newbridge-on-Wye
  Powys 20 E3
New Buckenham
  Norfk 25 H6
Newburgh Abers 61 G6
Newburgh Fife 51 G5
Newbury W Berk 14 C6
Newby Bridge Cumb ... 37 G5
Newcastle Emlyn
  Carmth 18 F3
Newcastleton Border ... 42 C3
Newcastle-under-
  Lyme Staffs 28 F5
Newcastle upon
  Tyne N u Ty 43 K5
New Cumnock E Ayrs .. 45 J6
New Deer Abers 60 F5
Newent Gloucs 21 L7
Newgale Pembks 18 C4

New Galloway D & G 41 G4
New Grimsby IoS 2 a1
Newhaven E Susx 10 C7
New Holland N Linc ... 35 G4
Newick E Susx 10 C6
New Luce D & G 40 C5
Newlyn Cnwll 2 B7
Newmains N Lans 45 L3
Newmarket Suffk 16 E2
Newmill Moray 60 B4
New Milton Hants 8 C6
Newnham Worcs 21 K4
Newnham on
  Severn Gloucs 13 G1
New Pitsligo Abers ... 60 F4
Newport Essex 16 D4
Newport IoW 8 E6
Newport Newpt 12 D3
Newport Pembks 18 D3
Newport Wrekin 28 E7
Newport-on-Tay Fife ... 51 J4
Newport Pagnell
  M Keyn 23 J6
New Quay Cerdgn 19 G1
Newquay Cnwll 2 E5
New Radnor Powys ... 20 F4
New Romney Kent 11 H5
Newsham N York 38 B3
Newton Abbot
  Devon 6 C5
Newton Aycliffe Dur ... 38 C2
Newton Ferrers
  Devon 3 L6
Newton Ferry W Isls .. 62 d8
Newtongrange
  Mdloth 46 D4
Newtonhill Abers 55 M5
Newton Mearns
  E Rens 45 J3
Newtonmore Highld ... 54 B4
Newton-on-the-
  Moor Nthumb 43 J2
Newton on Trent
  Lincs 30 E3
Newton St Cyres
  Devon 6 C3
Newton Solney
  Derbys 29 J7
Newton Stewart
  D & G 40 E5
Newtown Herefs 21 K5
Newtown Powys 20 F2
New Tredegar
  Caerph 12 C2
Newtyle Angus 51 H3
Neyland Pembks 18 D5
Nigg Highld 59 G3
Ninfield E Susx 10 E6
Niton IoW 8 F7
Nocton Lincs 31 G4
Norham Nthumb 47 J5
Normanton Wakefd ... 34 B4
Northall Bucks 15 G2
Northallerton N York .. 38 D4
Northam Devon 4 D4
Northampton
  Nhants 23 H4
North Berwick E Loth .. 46 F2
North Cave E R Yk 34 F4
Northchapel W Susx ... 9 J3
North Chideock
  Dorset 7 G3
North Cotes Lincs 35 K6
North Creake Norfk 24 F3
North Curry Somset ... 12 D8
North Dalton E R Yk ... 34 F2
North Elmham Norfk ... 25 G4
North Ferriby E R Yk ... 35 G4
Northfleet Kent 10 E2
North Frodingham
  E R Yk 35 H2
North Grimston
  N York 34 F1
North Hayling Hants ... 9 G5
North Hykeham
  Lincs 30 F3
Northiam E Susx 11 G6
North Kessock
  Highld 58 F4
North Kilworth Leics ... 23 G3
North Kyme Lincs 31 H4
Northleach Gloucs 22 C8
North Luffenham
  Rutlnd 23 J1
North Molton Devon ... 5 G4
North Muskham
  Notts 30 E4
Northop Flints 27 K3
North Petherton
  Somset 12 D7
North Rigton N York ... 33 L2
North Shields N Tyne ... 43 K5

North Somercotes
  Lincs 35 K6
North Walsham
  Norfk 25 J3
North Waltham Hants ... 8 F2
North Weald Bassett
  Essex 16 D6
Northwich Ches W 28 D3
North Wingfield
  Derbys 29 K4
Northwold Norfk 24 E6
Norton-on-Derwent
  N York 39 G6
Norton St Philip
  Somset 13 H5
Norwich Norfk 25 J5
Nottingham C Nott 30 C5
Nuneaton Warwks 22 E2
Nunney Somset 13 H6
Nutley E Susx 10 C5

O

Oadby Leics 23 G3
Oakham Rutlnd 30 E8
Oakhill Somset 13 G6
Oakley Bed 23 K5
Oakley Bucks 14 D3
Oakley Hants 8 F2
Oare Wilts 13 L5
Oban Ag & B 52 F7
Ochiltree E Ayrs 45 H5
Ockbrook Derbys 29 L6
Ockley Surrey 9 L2
Odiham Hants 9 G2
Offenham Worcs 22 B5
Ogbourne St George
  Wilts 13 M4
Ogmore-by-Sea
  V Glam 19 L8
Okehampton Devon 4 E7
Old Deer Abers 61 G4
Old Grimsby IoS 2 a1
Oldham Oldham 33 H6
Old Hurst Cambs 24 A7
Old Leake Lincs 31 K5
Oldmeldrum Abers ... 60 F6
Old Rayne Abers 60 D6
Old Sodbury S Glos ... 13 H3
Old Stratford Nhants ... 23 H6
Old Town IoS 2 b2
Old Windsor W & M ... 15 G6
Ollaberry Shet 61 b3
Ollerton Notts 30 C3
Olney M Keyn 23 J5
Ombersley Worcs 21 M4
Onchan IoM 36 c3
Onich Highld 53 G5
Orford Suffk 17 L3
Ormesby St
  Margaret Norfk ... 25 L4
Ormskirk Lancs 32 D6
Orpington Gt Lon 10 D2
Orsett Thurr 10 E1
Orton Cumb 37 J3
Osbournby Lincs 31 G6
Osmington Dorset 7 K4
Osmotherley N York ... 38 E4
Ospringe Kent 11 H3
Ossett Wakefd 33 L5
Oswaldkirk N York 38 F5
Oswestry Shrops 27 L6
Otford Kent 10 D3
Othery Somset 12 E7
Otley Leeds 33 K3
Otterbourne Hants 8 E4
Otterburn Nthumb 43 G3
Otter Ferry Ag & B ... 49 H5
Ottershaw Surrey 15 G7
Otterton Devon 6 E4
Ottery St Mary
  Devon 6 E3
Oundle Nhants 23 K2
Outwell Norfk 24 C5
Overseal Derbys 29 K7
Overton Hants 8 F2
Overton Wrexhm 28 B5
Ower Hants 8 D4
Oxford Oxon 14 C3
Oxted Surrey 10 C3
Oxton Notts 30 C5
Oxwich Swans 19 H7

P

Padbury Bucks 23 H7
Paddock Wood Kent .. 10 E4
Padiham Lancs 33 G4

Padstow Cnwll 2 F4
Paignton Torbay 6 C5
Pailton Warwks 22 F3
Painswick Gloucs 13 J1
Paisley Rens 45 J3
Palnackie D & G 41 J6
Pandy Mons 21 G7
Pangbourne W Berk ... 14 D6
Pannal N York 33 L2
Pant-y-dwr Powys 20 E3
Papworth Everard
  Cambs 16 B2
Parracombe Devon 4 F3
Pateley Bridge
  N York 38 B6
Patna E Ayrs 45 H6
Patrick IoM 36 b3
Patrington E R Yk 35 J4
Patterdale Cumb 37 G2
Pattishall Nhants 23 G5
Paulton BaNES 13 G5
Peacehaven E Susx ... 10 C7
Peasedown St John
  BaNES 13 H5
Peasmarsh E Susx 11 G6
Peebles Border 46 C5
Peel IoM 36 b3
Pelynt Cnwll 3 H5
Pembrey Carmth 19 G6
Pembridge Herefs 21 H4
Pembroke Pembks 18 D6
Pembroke Dock
  Pembks 18 D6
Pembury Kent 10 E4
Penally Pembks 18 E6
Penarth V Glam 12 C4
Pencoed Brdgnd 12 A3
Pencraig Herefs 21 J7
Pendine Carmth 18 F5
Pendock Worcs 21 L6
Pendoggett Cnwll 3 G3
Pengam Caerph 12 C2
Penicuik Mdloth 46 C4
Penistone Barns 33 L6
Penkridge Staffs 29 G7
Penmachno Conwy 27 G5
Penmaenmawr
  Conwy 26 F3
Pennal Gwynd 20 B1
Pennan Abers 60 F3
Penpont D & G 41 J3
Penrhyndeudraeth
  Gwynd 26 E6
Penrith Cumb 42 D8
Penryn Cnwll 2 E7
Pensford BaNES 13 G5
Penshurst Kent 10 D4
Pensilva Cnwll 3 J4
Pentewan Cnwll 2 F6
Pentraeth IoA 26 D3
Pentrefoelas Conwy ... 27 G5
Penybont Powys 20 F4
Pen-y-bont-fawr
  Powys 27 J7
Penygroes Gwynd 26 D4
Penzance Cnwll 2 B7
Perranporth Cnwll 2 D5
Pershore Worcs 22 A5
Perth P & K 50 F4
Peterborough C Pete ... 23 M1
Peterchurch Herefs ... 21 H6
Peterculter C Aber ... 55 L4
Peterhead Abers 61 H5
Peterlee Dur 43 L7
Petersfield Hants 9 H4
Petton Devon 5 J5
Petworth W Susx 9 J4
Pevensey E Susx 10 E7
Pewsey Wilts 13 L5
Pickering N York 39 G5
Piercebridge Darltn ... 38 C2
Pierowall Ork 65 C1
Pillaton Cnwll 3 J4
Pillerton Priors
  Warwks 22 D5
Pilling Lancs 32 D3
Pinchbeck Lincs 31 H7
Pinwherry S Ayrs 40 C3
Pinxton Derbys 29 L4
Pirbright Surrey 15 G7
Pitcaple Abers 60 E6
Pitlochry P & K 50 E2
Pitmedden Abers 60 F6
Pittenweem Fife 51 K6
Pleasley Derbys 30 B4
Plockton Highld 57 H6
Pluckley Kent 11 G4
Plumpton E Susx 10 C6
Plumtree Notts 30 C6
Plymouth C Plym 3 K5
Plympton C Plym 3 L5
Pocklington E R Yk ... 34 E2

Polbathic Cnwll 3 J5
Polegate E Susx............10 D7
Polmont Falk 50 E8
Polperro Cnwll...............3 H5
Polruan Cnwll..................3 G5
Polzeath Cnwll................2 F3
Pontardawe Neath..........19 K6
Pontardulais
  Swans.....................19 J6
Pontefract Wakefd 34 B5
Ponteland Nthumb.........43 J4
Ponterwyd Cerdgn 20 C3
Pontesbury Shrops 28 B8
Pontllanfraith
  Caerph...................12 C2
Pontrhydfendigaid
  Cerdgn....................19 K1
Pontrilas Herefs 21 H7
Pontyates Carmth 19 H5
Pontyberem Carmth 19 H5
Pontypool Torfn...........12 D2
Pontypridd Rhondd.......12 B3
Pool Leeds.................33 L3
Poole Poole..................8 A6
Poolewe Highld 57 H2
Pooley Bridge Cumb....37 H2
Porlock Somset 5 H3
Porlock Weir Somset....5 H3
Port Appin Ag & B........52 F6
Port Askaig Ag & B.......48 D6
Portavadie Ag & B.........49 H6
Port Bannatyne
  Ag & B.....................49 J6
Port Carlisle Cumb.......42 A5
Port Charlotte
  Ag & B.....................48 B7
Portchester Hants 8 F5
Port Ellen Ag & B..........48 C8
Port Erin IoM 36 a4
Portesham Dorset 7 J3
Port Eynon Swans........19 H7
Port Glasgow Inver.......49 L5
Portgordon Moray.........60 B3
Porth Rhondd...............12 B3
Porthcawl Brdgnd 19 L8
Porthcothan Cnwll..........2 E4
Porthcurno Cnwll............2 A8
Port Henderson
  Highld......................57 G3
Porthleven Cnwll.............2 C7
Porthmadog Gwynd.......26 E6
Porthtowan Cnwll............2 D6
Portinscale Cumb..........36 F2
Port Isaac Cnwll..............2 F3
Portishead N Som.........12 F4
Portlethen Abers...........55 M5
Portloe Cnwll..................2 F6
Port Logan D & G.........40 C7
Portmahomack
  Highld......................59 H2
Portnacroish Ag & B.....53 G6
Portnahaven Ag & B......48 A7
Port nan Long W Isls....62 d8
Port Nis W Isls.............62 i1
Port of Menteith
  Stirlg.......................50 B6
Port of Ness W Isls.......62 i1
Portpatrick D & G.........40 B6
Portreath Cnwll...............2 C6
Portree Highld..............56 E5
Port St Mary IoM...........36 a4
Portscatho Cnwll.............2 F7
Portskerra Highld...........64 D3
Portslade-by-Sea
  Br & H.....................10 B7
Portsmouth C Port.........9 G5
Portsoy Abers...............60 D3
Port Talbot Neath.........19 K7
Port William D & G.......40 E7
Postbridge Devon............3 M3
Postcombe Oxon...........14 E4
Potterne Wilts...............13 K5
Potters Bar Herts..........15 J4
Potton C Beds...............16 B3
Poulton-le-Fylde
  Lancs......................32 C3
Powburn Nthumb..........47 K7
Powick Worcs...............21 M5
Poynton Ches E............28 F2
Praa Sands Cnwll...........2 C7
Prees Shrops................28 C6
Preesall Lancs..............32 D3
Prees Green Shrops.....28 C6
Prenteg Gwynd.............26 E5
Prestatyn Denbgs.........27 H1
Prestbury Ches E..........28 F3
Presteigne Powys.........21 G4
Preston Border.............47 H4
Preston Lancs...............32 E4
Preston Candover
  Hants........................8 F2

Preston Capes
  Nhants....................22 F5
Prestonpans E Loth......46 E3
Prestwich Bury.............33 G6
Prestwick S Ayrs..........45 G5
Prestwood Bucks.........14 F4
Priddy Somset.............12 F6
Princes Risborough
  Bucks.....................14 F4
Princethorpe Warwks...22 E3
Princetown Devon..........3 L4
Prospect Cumb............41 L7
Prudhoe Nthumb..........43 H5
Pucklechurch S Glos....13 H4
Puddletown Dorset........7 K3
Pudsey Leeds..............33 L4
Pulborough W Susx.......9 K4
Pulford Ches W............28 B4
Pulham St Mary
  Norfk......................25 J7
Pumsaint Carmth.........19 J3
Purfleet Thurr..............10 D1
Purton Wilts.................13 L3
Pwll Carmth.................19 H6
Pwllheli Gwynd............26 C6
Pyecombe W Susx.......10 B6
Pyle Brdgnd.................19 L7

Q

Quatt Shrops...............21 L2
Queensferry Flints.......27 L3
Quendon Essex...........16 D4

R

Rackenford Devon..........5 H5
Rackheath Norfk...........25 J4
Radcliffe on Trent
  Notts......................30 C6
Radlett Herts...............15 H4
Radstock BaNES..........13 G5
Radwinter Essex..........16 E4
Radyr Cardif................12 C4
Rafford Moray..............59 J4
Raglan Mons................12 E1
Rainham Gt Lon...........10 D1
Rainham Medway.........10 F2
Rampside Cumb...........36 F6
Ramsbottom Bury.........33 G5
Ramsbury Wilts............14 A6
Ramsey Cambs............24 A7
Ramsey IoM.................36 c2
Ramsgate Kent............11 L2
Rannoch Station
  P & K......................53 L5
Rapness Ork................65 c2
Rathen Abers...............61 G3
Rattray P & K...............51 G3
Raunds Nhants............23 K3
Ravenglass Cumb.........36 E4
Ravenscar N York.........39 J3
Ravenstonedale
  Cumb......................37 K3
Rawmarsh Rothm.........34 B7
Rawtenstall Lancs.........33 G4
Rayleigh Essex............16 F7
Reading Readg.............14 E6
Reay Highld.................64 F2
Reculver Kent..............11 K2
Redbourn Herts............15 H3
Redbrook Gloucs..........12 F1
Redbrook Wrexhm........28 C5
Redcar R & Cl..............38 F2
Redditch Worcs............22 B4
Redgrave Suffk.............25 G7
Redhill N Som..............12 F5
Redhill Surrey..............10 B4
Redmile Leics..............30 E6
Rednal Shrops..............28 B6
Red Roses Carmth........18 F5
Red Row Nthumb..........43 K2
Redruth Cnwll................2 D6
Red Wharf Bay IoA......26 D2
Reedham Norfk............25 L5
Reepham Norfk............25 H4
Reighton N York...........39 K5
Rempstone Notts..........30 C7
Renfrew Rens...............45 H2
Renwick Cumb.............42 D7
Repton Derbys..............29 K6
Resolven Neath............19 L6
Retford Notts...............30 D2
Reynoldston Swans......19 H8
Rhayader Powys...........20 D4
Rhiconich Highld...........63 H3
Rhoose V Glam..............5 J2

Rhosllanerchrugog
  Wrexhm....................27 L5
Rhosneigr IoA..............26 C3
Rhôs-on-Sea Conwy....27 G2
Rhossili Swans.............19 G7
Rhu Ag & B..................49 L5
Rhuddlan Denbgs.........27 J3
Rhyd-Ddu Gwynd.........26 E4
Rhydowen Cerdgn........19 G2
Rhyl Denbgs.................27 H2
Rhymney Caerph..........12 C1
Richards Castle
  Herefs.....................21 J4
Richmond Gt Lon..........15 J6
Richmond N York..........38 B3
Rickmansworth
  Herts.......................15 H4
Riding Mill Nthumb.......43 H5
Ridsdale Nthumb..........43 G4
Rillington N York...........39 H5
Ringford D & G.............41 G6
Ringmer E Susx...........10 C8
Ringwood Hants.............8 C5
Ripley Derbys...............29 K5
Ripley N York................38 C7
Ripley Surrey................15 H7
Ripon N York................38 D6
Ripple Worcs................21 M6
Ripponden Calder.........33 J5
Risca Caerph................12 D3
Risegate Lincs..............31 H6
Riseley Bed..................23 K4
Riseley Wokham...........14 E7
Risley Derbys...............29 L6
Risley Warrtn...............32 F7
Roade Nhants..............23 H5
Roberton Border...........46 E7
Roberton S Lans...........45 M5
Robertsbridge E Susx...10 F6
Robeston Wathen
  Pembks....................18 E5
Robin Hood's Bay
  N York.....................39 J3
Rocester Staffs.............29 H6
Roch Pembks...............18 C4
Rochdale Rochdl...........33 H5
Roche Cnwll...................2 F5
Rochester Medway.......10 F2
Rochester Nthumb........42 F3
Rochford Essex............17 G7
Rock Cnwll....................2 F3
Rockcliffe Cumb...........42 B5
Rockcliffe D & G...........41 J6
Rockingham Nhants......23 J2
Rogate W Susx...............9 H4
Rogerstone Newpt.......12 D3
Rollesby Norfk..............25 L4
Rolvenden Kent............11 G5
Romaldkirk Dur............37 M2
Romanno Bridge
  Border......................46 C5
Romford Gt Lon............16 D7
Romsey Hants................8 D4
Rookhope Dur...............43 G7
Ropley Hants..................9 G3
Rosedale Abbey
  N York.....................39 G4
Rosehall Highld............63 K7
Rosehearty Abers.........61 G3
Rosemarkie Highld........58 F4
Rosewell Mdloth...........46 B4
Rossett Wrexhm...........28 B4
Ross-on-Wye Herefs....21 K7
Rosyth Fife..................46 B2
Rothbury Nthumb.........43 J4
Rotherfield E Susx........10 D5
Rotherham Rothm.........34 B7
Rothes Moray...............59 L4
Rothesay Ag & B..........49 J6
Rothwell Leeds.............33 M4
Rothwell Nhants...........23 H3
Rottingdean Br & H......10 C7
Roughton Norfk............25 J3
Rowland's Castle
  Hants........................9 G5
Rowlands Gill Gatesd....43 J6
Rowsley Derbys............29 J3
Roxburgh Border..........47 G6
Roxwell Essex..............16 E6
Royal Leamington
  Spa Warwks.............22 D4
Royal Sutton
  Coldfield Birm..........22 C2
Royal Tunbridge
  Wells Kent...............10 E3
Royal Wootton
  Bassett Wilts...........13 L3
Royston Barns.............34 A5
Royston Herts..............16 C4
Rozel Jersey.................7 c1
Ruabon Wrexhm...........27 L5
Ruddington Notts..........30 C6

Rudgwick W Susx..........9 K3
Rudston E R Yk............39 K6
Rufford Lancs...............32 D5
Rugby Warwks..............22 F3
Rugeley Staffs..............29 G7
Rumbling Bridge
  P & K......................50 F6
Runcorn Halton............28 C2
Rushden Nhants............23 K4
Rushyford Dur...............38 C1
Ruskington Lincs..........31 G5
Rustington W Susx..........9 K5
Ruswarp N York............39 H3
Rutherglen S Lans.........45 J2
Ruthin Denbgs..............27 J4
Ruyton-XI-Towns
  Shrops....................28 B7
Rydal Cumb.................37 G3
Ryde IoW......................8 F6
Rye E Susx..................11 G6

S

Saddell Ag & B.............44 B5
Saffron Walden
  Essex.....................16 D4
St Abbs Border.............47 J3
St Agnes Cnwll..............2 D5
St Albans Herts............15 H3
St Andrew Guern............6 a2
St Andrews Fife...........51 K5
St Arvans Mons...........12 F2
St Asaph Denbgs..........27 J3
St Athan V Glam............5 J1
St Aubin Jersey.............7 b2
St Austell Cnwll.............2 F5
St Bees Cumb..............36 D3
St Blazey Cnwll..............3 G5
St Boswells Border.......46 F6
St Brelade Jersey...........7 a2
St Brelade's Bay
  Jersey.......................7 a2
St Briavels Gloucs........12 F2
St Buryan Cnwll..............2 A7
St Catherines Ag & B.....49 J3
St Clears Carmth..........18 F5
St Cleer Cnwll................3 H4
St Clement Jersey...........7 c2
St Columb Major
  Cnwll........................2 F4
St Combs Abers............61 H3
St Cyrus Abers.............55 K7
St Davids Pembks.........18 B4
St Day Cnwll..................2 D6
St Dogmaels Pembks....18 E2
St Fergus Abers............61 H4
St Fillans P & K.............50 C4
St Florence Pembks......18 E6
St Helens IoW................9 G6
St Helens St Hel...........32 E7
St Helier Jersey.............7 b2
St Ives Cambs..............24 A8
St Ives Cnwll.................2 B6
St John Jersey..............7 b1
St John's IoM...............36 b3
St John's Chapel Dur....43 G7
St John's Town of
  Dalry D & G..............41 G4
St Jude's IoM...............36 c2
St Just Cnwll..................2 A7
St Just-in-Roseland
  Cnwll........................2 E7
St Keverne Cnwll............2 E8
St Keyne Cnwll...............3 H5
St Lawrence IoW............8 F7
St Lawrence Jersey.......7 b1
St Leonards S Lans.......10 F7
St Margaret's at
  Cliffe Kent...............11 L4
St Margaret's Hope
  Ork..........................65 c5
St Marks IoM...............36 b3
St Martin Guern.............6 b2
St Martin Jersey.............7 c1
St Mary Jersey..............7 b1
St Mary's Ork...............65 c4
St Mary's Bay Kent.......11 J5
St Mawes Cnwll.............2 E7
St Mawgan Cnwll...........2 E4
St Monans Fife.............51 K6
St Neots Cambs...........23 M4
St Osyth Essex.............17 J5
St Ouen Jersey..............7 a1
St Owens Cross
  Herefs.....................21 J7
St Peter Jersey.............7 b1
St Peter Port Guern.......6 b2
St Peter's Guern............6 a2
St Sampson Guern.........6 b1
St Saviour Guern...........6 b1

St Saviour Jersey.........7 b2
St Stephen Cnwll.........2 F5
St Tudy Cnwll.........3 G3
Salcombe Devon.........6 B7
Sale Traffd.........33 G7
Salen Ag & B.........52 D6
Salen Highld.........52 E4
Salford Salfd.........33 G6
Salfords Surrey.........10 B4
Saline Fife.........50 F7
Salisbury Wilts.........8 C3
Saltash Cnwll.........3 K5
Saltburn-by-the-Sea
  R & Cl.........38 F2
Saltcoats N Ayrs.........44 F4
Saltfleet Lincs.........35 K7
Sampford Arundel
  Somset.........5 K5
Sanaigmore Ag & B.........48 B6
Sandbach Ches E.........28 E4
Sandbank Ag & B.........49 K5
Sandford-on-
  Thames Oxon.........14 C4
Sandhaven Abers.........61 G3
Sandhead D & G.........40 C6
Sandhurst Br For.........14 F7
Sandness Shet.........61 a5
Sandon Staffs.........29 G6
Sandown IoW.........8 F7
Sandridge Herts.........15 J3
Sandsend N York.........39 H3
Sandwich Kent.........11 L3
Sandwick Shet.........61 c7
Sandy C Beds.........23 L5
Sanquhar D & G.........45 L6
Sarn Gwynd.........26 B6
Sarre Kent.........11 K2
Saundby Notts.........34 E7
Saundersfoot
  Pembks.........18 E5
Saunton Devon.........4 D4
Sawbridgeworth
  Herts.........16 D5
Sawston Cambs.........16 D3
Sawtry Cambs.........23 L3
Saxby Leics.........30 E7
Saxilby Lincs.........30 E3
Saxmundham Suffk.........17 L2
Saxthorpe Norfk.........25 H3
Scalasaig Ag & B.........48 C4
Scalby N York.........39 J4
Scalloway Shet.........61 c6
Scamblesby Lincs.........31 J3
Scarborough N York.........39 K4
Scarinish Ag & B.........48 b2
Scawby N Linc.........34 F6
Scole Norfk.........25 H7
Scone P & K.........51 G4
Sconser Highld.........56 E6
Scotch Corner N York.........38 C3
Scotter Lincs.........34 F6
Scotton N York.........38 B4
Scoulton Norfk.........25 G5
Scourie Highld.........63 G4
Scrabster Highld.........65 G2
Scunthorpe N Linc.........34 F5
Seaford E Susx.........10 D7
Seaham Dur.........43 L6
Seahouses Nthumb.........47 L6
Seal Kent.........10 D3
Seamer N York.........39 J5
Sea Palling Norfk.........25 L3
Seascale Cumb.........36 D3
Seathwaite Cumb.........36 F4
Seaton Cumb.........41 K8
Seaton Devon.........6 F3
Seaton Delaval
  Nthumb.........43 K4
Seave Green N York.........38 F4
Seaview IoW.........9 G6
Sedbergh Cumb.........37 J4
Sedgeberrow Worcs.........22 B6
Sedgebrook Lincs.........30 E6
Sedgefield Dur.........38 D1
Sedlescombe E Susx.........10 F6
Seend Wilts.........13 K5
Selborne Hants.........9 G3
Selby N York.........34 D4
Selkirk Border.........46 E6
Sellindge Kent.........11 J4
Selsey W Susx.........9 H6
Selston Notts.........29 L4
Send Surrey.........15 G7
Sennen Cnwll.........2 A7
Sennybridge Powys.........20 D7
Setchey Norfk.........24 D4
Settle N York.........37 L6
Sevenoaks Kent.........10 D3
Seven Sisters Neath.........19 L5
Shaftesbury Dorset.........13 J8
Shalford Essex.........16 F4
Shalford Surrey.........9 K2

Shandon Ag & B.........49 K5
Shanklin IoW.........8 F7
Shap Cumb.........37 H2
Shardlow Derbys.........29 L6
Sharnbrook Bed.........23 K4
Sharpness Gloucs.........13 G2
Shaugh Prior Devon.........3 L4
Shavington Ches E.........28 E5
Shawbury Shrops.........28 C7
Shebbear Devon.........4 D6
Sheepwash Devon.........4 E6
Sheerness Kent.........11 G2
Sheffield Sheff.........29 K2
Shefford C Beds.........23 L6
Shepreth Cambs.........16 C3
Shepshed Leics.........30 B7
Shepton Mallet
  Somset.........13 G6
Sherborne Dorset.........7 J1
Sherburn N York.........39 J5
Sherburn in Elmet
  N York.........34 C4
Sherfield on Loddon
  Hants.........14 D7
Sheriff Hutton
  N York.........38 F6
Sheringham Norfk.........25 H2
Shiel Bridge Highld.........57 J7
Shieldaig Highld.........57 H4
Shifnal Shrops.........28 E8
Shildon Dur.........38 C2
Shillingford Oxon.........14 D4
Shillingstone Dorset.........7 L2
Shinfield Wokham.........14 E6
Shinness Highld.........63 K6
Shipdham Norfk.........25 G5
Shiplake Oxon.........14 E6
Shipley C Brad.........33 K3
Shipston-on-Stour
  Warwks.........22 D6
Shipton N York.........38 E7
Shiptonthorpe
  E R Yk.........34 E3
Shirebrook Derbys.........30 B3
Shoeburyness
  Sthend.........17 G8
Shoreham-by-Sea
  W Susx.........9 L5
Shorwell IoW.........8 E7
Shotley Suffk.........17 K4
Shottisham Suffk.........17 L3
Shotts N Lans.........45 L2
Shrewsbury Shrops.........28 C8
Shrewton Wilts.........13 L6
Shrivenham Oxon.........13 M3
Shurdington Gloucs.........22 A7
Shute Devon.........6 F3
Sible Hedingham
  Essex.........16 F4
Sibsey Lincs.........31 J5
Sibson Leics.........22 E1
Sidmouth Devon.........6 E3
Silchester Hants.........14 D7
Sileby Leics.........30 C7
Silk Willoughby Lincs.........31 G5
Silloth Cumb.........41 L6
Silsoe C Beds.........23 L6
Silverdale Lancs.........37 H5
Silver End Essex.........16 F5
Silverstone Nhants.........23 G6
Silverton Devon.........5 H6
Simonburn Nthumb.........42 F4
Simonsbath Somset.........5 G4
Singleton W Susx.........9 J4
Sissinghurst Kent.........10 F4
Sittingbourne Kent.........11 G3
Sixpenny Handley
  Dorset.........8 A4
Skegness Lincs.........31 L4
Skellingthorpe Lincs.........30 F3
Skelmersdale Lancs.........32 D6
Skelmorlie N Ayrs.........49 K6
Skelton Cumb.........42 C7
Skelton R & Cl.........38 F2
Skenfrith Mons.........21 H7
Skerray Highld.........64 C2
Skipness Ag & B.........44 C3
Skipsea E R Yk.........35 H2
Skipton N York.........33 J2
Skirling Border.........46 B6
Skirwith Cumb.........42 D8
Slaidburn Lancs.........32 F2
Slaley Nthumb.........43 G6
Slamannan Falk.........45 L1
Slapton Devon.........5 G5
Sleaford Lincs.........31 G5
Sledmere E R Yk.........39 J6
Sleights N York.........39 H3
Slingsby N York.........39 G5
Slough Slough.........15 G5
Smailholm Border.........47 G6
Smarden Kent.........11 G4

Smithfield Cumb.........42 C5
Snainton N York.........39 J5
Snape Suffk.........17 L2
Snettisham Norfk.........24 E3
Snodland Kent.........10 E3
Soham Cambs.........24 D7
Solihull Solhll.........22 C3
Solva Pembks.........18 B4
Somersham Cambs.........24 B7
Somerton Somset.........12 F7
Sompting W Susx.........9 L5
Sonning Wokham.........14 E6
Sonning Common
  Oxon.........14 E5
Sorbie D & G.........40 E6
Soulby Cumb.........37 K3
Souldern Oxon.........22 F6
Souldrop Bed.........23 K4
Sourton Devon.........3 L2
Southam Warwks.........22 E4
Southampton C Sotn.........8 E5
South Benfleet Essex.........16 F8
Southborough Kent.........10 D4
South Brent Devon.........6 A5
South Cave E R Yk.........34 F4
South Elmsall Wakefd.........34 B5
Southend Ag & B.........44 B6
Southend-on-Sea
  Sthend.........17 G8
Southery Norfk.........24 D6
South Harting
  W Susx.........9 H4
South Hayling Hants.........9 G5
South Holmwood
  Surrey.........9 L2
South Kyme Lincs.........31 H5
South Mimms Herts.........15 J4
Southminster Essex.........17 H7
South Molton Devon.........4 F5
Southmoor Oxon.........14 B4
South Normanton
  Derbys.........29 L4
South Ockendon
  Thurr.........16 E8
South Petherton
  Somset.........7 G1
Southport Sefton.........32 C5
South Queensferry
  C Edin.........46 B3
South Raynham
  Norfk.........24 F4
Southrepps Norfk.........25 J3
Southsea C Port.........9 G6
South Shields S Tyne.........43 L5
South Stainley
  N York.........38 C6
South Walsham
  Norfk.........25 K4
Southwell Notts.........30 D4
Southwick Hants.........9 G5
Southwick W Susx.........10 B6
South Witham Lincs.........30 F7
Southwold Suffk.........25 L7
South Woodham
  Ferrers Essex.........16 F7
South Zeal Devon.........3 M2
Sowerby N York.........38 D5
Sowerby Bridge
  Calder.........33 J4
Spalding Lincs.........31 H7
Sparkford Somset.........13 G8
Sparsholt Hants.........8 E3
Spean Bridge Highld.........53 J3
Spennymoor Dur.........43 K7
Spetisbury Dorset.........7 L2
Spey Bay Moray.........60 B3
Spilsby Lincs.........31 K3
Spinningdale Highld.........58 F1
Spittal Highld.........65 H3
Spittal of Glenshee
  P & K.........54 E7
Spixworth Norfk.........25 J4
Spofforth N York.........34 A2
Springholm D & G.........41 H5
Sproatley E R Yk.........35 H4
Stadhampton Oxon.........14 D4
Stadhlaigearraidh
  W Isls.........62 c11
Staffin Highld.........56 E3
Stafford Staffs.........28 F7
Staindrop Dur.........38 B2
Staines-upon-
  Thames Surrey.........15 G6
Stainforth N York.........37 L6
Staithes N York.........39 G2
Stalham Norfk.........25 K4
Stalybridge Tamesd.........33 J6
Stamford Lincs.........31 G8
Stamford Bridge
  E R Yk.........39 G7
Stamfordham
  Nthumb.........43 H5

Standish Wigan.........32 E5
Standon Herts.........16 C5
Stanford in the Vale
  Oxon.........14 B4
Stanford le Hope
  Thurr.........10 E1
Stanhope Dur.........43 G7
Stanley Dur.........43 J6
Stanley P & K.........50 F4
Stannington Nthumb.........43 J4
Stansted
  Mountfitchet
  Essex.........16 D5
Stanton Suffk.........25 G7
Stanton St Quintin
  Wilts.........13 J4
Stanway Gloucs.........22 B6
Staple Fitzpaine
  Somset.........6 F1
Stapleford Notts.........30 B6
Staplehurst Kent.........10 F4
Starbotton N York.........37 M5
Staveley Cumb.........37 H4
Staveley Derbys.........29 L3
Staverton Nhants.........22 F4
Staxton N York.........39 J5
Steeple Essex.........17 G6
Steeple Aston Oxon.........22 F7
Steeple Bumpstead
  Essex.........16 E3
Stenhousemuir Falk.........50 D8
Steornabhagh W Isls.........62 h3
Stevenage Herts.........16 B5
Stevenston N Ayrs.........44 F4
Steventon Oxon.........14 C5
Stewarton E Ayrs.........45 H3
Stewkley Bucks.........23 J7
Steyning W Susx.........9 L5
Stibb Cross Devon.........4 D5
Stickford Lincs.........31 J4
Stickney Lincs.........31 J4
Stiffkey Norfk.........25 G2
Stilligarry W Isls.........62 c11
Stillington N York.........38 F6
Stilton Cambs.........23 L2
Stirling Stirlg.........50 D7
Stock Essex.........16 E7
Stockbridge Hants.........8 D3
Stockport Stockp.........33 H7
Stocksbridge Sheff.........33 L6
Stockton-on-Tees
  S on T.........38 E2
Stogursey Somset.........12 C6
Stoke-by-Clare Suffk.........16 F3
Stoke-by-Nayland
  Suffk.........17 H4
Stoke Canon Devon.........6 C6
Stoke Ferry Norfk.........24 E5
Stoke Fleming Devon.........6 C6
Stoke Gabriel Devon.........6 C6
Stoke Goldington
  M Keyn.........23 J5
Stoke Lacy Herefs.........21 K5
Stoke Mandeville
  Bucks.........14 F3
Stokenchurch Bucks.........14 E4
Stoke-on-Trent
  C Stke.........28 F5
Stoke Poges Bucks.........15 G5
Stokesley N York.........38 E3
Stone Staffs.........28 F6
Stonehaven Abers.........55 L5
Stonehouse Gloucs.........13 H2
Stonehouse S Lans.........45 K3
Stoneykirk D & G.........40 B6
Stonor Oxon.........14 E5
Stony Stratford
  M Keyn.........23 H6
Stornoway W Isls.........62 h3
Storrington W Susx.........9 K4
Stotfold C Beds.........16 A4
Stoulton Worcs.........22 A5
Stourbridge Dudley.........21 M3
Stourpaine Dorset.........7 L2
Stourport-on-
  Severn Worcs.........21 L3
Stourton Staffs.........21 M2
Stow Border.........46 E5
Stow-cum-Quy
  Cambs.........16 D2
Stowmarket Suffk.........17 H2
Stow-on-the-Wold
  Gloucs.........22 C7
Strachan Abers.........55 K5
Strachur Ag & B.........49 J3
Stradbroke Suffk.........25 J7
Stradishall Suffk.........16 F3
Stradsett Norfk.........24 D5
Straiton S Ayrs.........45 G7
Stranraer D & G.........40 B5
Stratfield Turgis
  Hants.........14 E7

Stratford Gt Lon 16 C8
Stratford St Andrew
Suffk 17 L2
Stratford-upon-
Avon Warwks 22 C5
Strathaven S Lans 45 K4
Strathblane Stirlg 50 B8
Strathcanaird Highld 63 G7
Strathdon Abers 55 G3
Strathpeffer Highld 58 D4
Strathy Highld 64 E2
Strathyre Stirlg 50 B5
Stratton Cnwll 4 B6
Stratton-on-the-
Fosse Somset 13 G6
Streatley W Berk 14 D5
Street Somset 12 F7
Strensall C York 38 F7
Strete Devon 6 C6
Stretford Traffd 33 G7
Stretham Cambs 24 C7
Stretton Rutlnd 30 F7
Strichen Abers 61 G4
Stromeferry Highld 57 H5
Stromness Ork 65 b4
Stronachlachar Stirlg 49 M3
Strone Ag & B 49 K5
Strontian Highld 52 F5
Strood Medway 10 F2
Stroud Gloucs 13 J2
Struy Highld 58 C5
Stuartfield Abers 61 G5
Studland Dorset 8 B7
Studley Warwks 22 B4
Sturminster Newton
Dorset 7 K1
Sturry Kent 11 J3
Sturton by Stow Lincs ..30 E2
Sudbury Derbys 29 H6
Sudbury Suffk 17 G3
Sulby IoM 36 c2
Summercourt Cnwll 2 E5
Sunbury-on-Thames
Surrey 15 H6
Sunderland Sundld 43 L6
Surfleet Lincs 31 H6
Sutterton Lincs 31 J6
Sutton Cambs 24 C7
Sutton Gt Lon 10 B2
Sutton Benger Wilts 13 K4
Sutton Bridge Lincs 24 C4
Sutton Coldfield
Birm 22 C2
Sutton Courtenay
Oxon 14 C4
Sutton-in-Ashfield
Notts 30 B4
Sutton on Sea Lincs 31 L2
Sutton-on-the-
Forest N York 38 F6
Sutton on Trent
Notts 30 E3
Sutton Scotney
Hants 8 E2
Sutton Valence Kent ...10 F4
Swadlincote Derbys 29 K7
Swaffham Norfk 24 F5
Swainswick BaNES 13 H4
Swalcliffe Oxon 22 E6
Swallow Lincs 35 H6
Swallowfield
Wokham 14 E7
Swanage Dorset 8 B7
Swanley Kent 10 D2
Swansea Swans 19 J6
Swanwick Derbys 29 K4
Swanwick Hants 8 F5
Swaton Lincs 31 G6
Swavesey Cambs 16 C1
Sway Hants 8 D6
Swindon Swindn 13 L3
Swineshead Bed 23 K4
Swineshead Lincs 31 H5
Swinford Leics 22 F3
Swinton Border 47 H5
Swinton Rothm 34 B6
Syderstone Norfk 24 F3
Symbister Shet 61 d4
Symington S Ayrs 45 G5
Symington S Lans 46 A6
Symonds Yat (West)
Herefs 21 J8
Syresham Nhants 23 G6
Syston Leics 30 C8

Tadcaster N York 34 B3
Tadley Hants 14 D7
Tain Highld 59 G2

Tairbeart W Isls 62 f6
Talgarreg Cerdgn 19 G2
Talgarth Powys 20 F6
Talladale Highld 57 J3
Talley Carmth 19 J3
Talmine Highld 64 C2
Tal-y-bont Cerdgn 20 B2
Tal-y-Bont Gwynd 26 E6
Tal-y-Bont Conwy 26 F3
Tal-y-bont Gwynd 26 E7
Tal-y-Cafn Conwy 27 G3
Tamworth Staffs 22 C1
Tannadice Angus 51 J2
Tan-y-groes Cerdgn 18 F2
Taplow Bucks 14 F5
Tarbert Ag & B 49 G6
Tarbert W Isls 62 f6
Tarbet Ag & B 49 L3
Tarbolton S Ayrs 45 H5
Tarland Abers 55 H4
Tarleton Lancs 32 D5
Tarporley Ches W 28 C4
Tarrant Hinton
Dorset 7 M2
Tarskavaig Highld 56 F7
Tarves Abers 60 F6
Tarvin Ches W 28 C3
Tattershall Lincs 31 H4
Taunton Somset 12 D8
Taverham Norfk 25 H4
Tavistock Devon 3 K4
Tayinloan Ag & B 44 B3
Taynton Oxon 22 D8
Taynuilt Ag & B 53 G7
Tayport Fife 51 J4
Tayvallich Ag & B 48 F5
Tebay Cumb 37 J3
Tedburn St Mary
Devon 6 B3
Teddington Gloucs 22 A6
Teignmouth Devon 6 C4
Telford Wrekin 28 E8
Temple Mdloth 46 D4
Temple Bar Cerdgn 19 H2
Templecombe
Somset 13 H8
Temple Sowerby
Cumb 37 J1
Tempsford C Beds 23 L5
Tenbury Wells Worcs ...21 K4
Tenby Pembks 18 E6
Tenterden Kent 11 G5
Ternhill Shrops 28 D6
Terrington St
Clement Norfk 24 C4
Tetbury Gloucs 13 J3
Tetford Lincs 31 J3
Tetney Lincs 35 J6
Tetsworth Oxon 14 E4
Teviothead Border 42 C2
Tewkesbury Gloucs 21 M6
Teynham Kent 11 H3
Thame Oxon 14 E3
Thatcham W Berk 14 C6
Thaxted Essex 16 E4
Theale W Berk 14 D6
Theberton Suffk 17 M2
The Bungalow IoM 36 c2
Thetford Norfk 24 F7
Theydon Bois Essex 16 C7
Thirsk N York 38 B5
Thornbury S Glos 13 G3
Thorne Donc 34 D5
Thorney C Pete 24 A5
Thornham Norfk 24 E2
Thornhill D & G 41 J3
Thornhill Stirlg 50 C6
Thornley Dur 43 L7
Thornton Fife 51 H6
Thornton-le-Dale
N York 39 H5
Thornton-le-Street
N York 38 D5
Thornton Watlass
N York 38 C5
Thorpe End Norfk 25 J5
Thorpe-le-Soken
Essex 17 J5
Thorpeness Suffk 17 M2
Thorrington Essex 17 J5
Thrapston Nhants 23 K3
Three Cocks Powys 20 F6
Threekingham Lincs 31 G6
Threlkeld Cumb 36 F2
Threshfield N York 37 M6
Thropton Nthumb 43 H2
Thrumster Highld 65 J4
Thurcroft Rothm 34 C7
Thurlestone Devon 6 A7
Thurnscoe Barns 34 B6
Thursby Cumb 42 B6
Thurso Highld 65 G2

Thurstaston Wirral 27 K2
Thurston Suffk 17 G2
Thwaite N York 37 L4
Tibshelf Derbys 29 L4
Ticehurst E Susx 10 E5
Tickhill Donc 34 C7
Ticknall Derbys 29 K7
Tideswell Derbys 29 H3
Tidworth Wilts 8 C2
Tigh a Ghearraidh
W Isls 62 c8
Tigharry W Isls 62 c8
Tilbury Thurr 10 E2
Tilford Surrey 9 J2
Tillicoultry Clacks 50 E6
Tilshead Wilts 13 K6
Tilstock Shrops 28 C6
Tilton on the Hill
Leics 30 D8
Tintagel Cnwll 3 G3
Tintern Parva Mons 12 F2
Tiptree Essex 17 G5
Tisbury Wilts 13 K7
Tissington Derbys 29 J5
Tittensor Staffs 28 F6
Tiverton Devon 5 H6
Tobermory Ag & B 52 C5
Toddington C Beds 23 K7
Todmorden Calder 33 H4
Toft Shet 61 c3
Toft Hill Dur 38 B1
Tolastadh W Isls 62 i2
Tollard Royal Wilts 7 M1
Tollesbury Essex 17 H6
Tolleshunt D'Arcy
Essex 17 G6
Tolpuddle Dorset 7 K3
Tolsta W Isls 62 i2
Tomatin Highld 59 G6
Tomintoul Moray 54 F3
Tomnavoulin Moray 59 K6
Tonbridge Kent 10 E4
Tongue Highld 64 C3
Tonypandy Rhondd 12 B3
Tonyrefail Rhondd 12 B3
Topcliffe N York 38 D5
Topsham Devon 6 D3
Torbeg N Ayrs 44 C5
Torcross Devon 6 B7
Tore Highld 58 E4
Torksey Lincs 30 E3
Torphichen W Loth 46 A3
Torphins Abers 55 J4
Torpoint Cnwll 3 K5
Torquay Torbay 6 C5
Torrance E Duns 45 J1
Torridon Highld 57 H4
Torrin Highld 56 F7
Torryburn Fife 46 B2
Torthorwald D & G 41 K4
Torver Cumb 36 F4
Totland IoW 8 C7
Totnes Devon 6 B5
Totton Hants 8 D6
Towcester Nhants 23 G5
Tow Law Dur 43 J7
Town Yetholm
Border 47 H6
Traquair Border 46 D6
Trawden Lancs 33 H3
Trawsfynydd Gwynd 26 F6
Trearddur Bay IoA 26 B2
Trecastle Powys 20 D7
Tredegar Blae G 12 C1
Treen Cnwll 2 A8
Trefriw Conwy 27 G4
Tregaron Cerdgn 19 J1
Tregony Cnwll 2 F6
Treherbert Rhondd 19 M6
Trellech Mons 12 F2
Tremadog Gwynd 26 E5
Trimdon Dur 43 L7
Trimingham Norfk 25 J3
Tring Herts 14 F3
Trinity Jersey 7 b1
Troon S Ayrs 45 G5
Trotton W Susx 9 H4
Troutbeck Cumb 37 G3
Trowbridge Wilts 13 J5
Truro Cnwll 2 E6
Tugby Leics 23 H1
Tullibody Clacks 50 D7
Tummel Bridge P & K ...50 D2
Tunbridge Wells Kent ...10 E4
Tunstall Staffs 17 L2
Turnberry S Ayrs 44 F7
Turnditch Derbys 29 K5
Turner's Hill W Susx 10 B5
Turriff Abers 60 E4
Turvey Bed 23 K5
Tutbury Staffs 29 J6
Tuxford Notts 30 D3

Twycross Leics 22 E1
Twyford Hants 8 E4
Twyford Wokham 14 E6
Twynholm D & G 41 G6
Tyndrum Stirlg 53 K7
Tynemouth N Tyne 43 L5
Tytherleigh Devon 6 F2
Tywyn Gwynd 20 A1

Uckfield E Susx 10 D6
Uffculme Devon 5 J6
Uffington Oxon 14 A5
Ugborough Devon 6 A6
Uig Highld 56 D3
Ulceby N Linc 35 H5
Uldale Cumb 42 A7
Ullapool Highld 63 G7
Ullenhall Warwks 22 C4
Ulpha Cumb 36 E4
Ulsta Shet 61 c3
Ulverston Cumb 36 F5
Umberleigh Devon 4 F7
Unapool Highld 63 H4
Upavon Wilts 13 L5
Uplyme Devon 6 F3
Upminster Gt Lon 10 D8
Upottery Devon 6 E2
Upper Beeding
W Susx 9 L5
Upper Benefield
Nhants 23 K2
Upper Broughton
Notts 30 D7
Upper Largo Fife 51 J6
Upper Lydbrook
Gloucs 21 K8
Upper Tean Staffs 29 G5
Uppingham Rutlnd 23 J1
Upstreet Kent 11 K3
Upton Snodsbury
Worcs 22 A5
Upton-upon-Severn
Worcs 21 M6
Urchfont Wilts 13 K5
Usk Mons 12 E2
Uttoxeter Staffs 29 G5
Uxbridge Gt Lon 15 H5
Uyeasound Shet 61 d2

Vale Guern 6 b1
Ventnor IoW 8 F7
Verwood Dorset 8 B5
Vidlin Shet 61 c4
Virginia Water Surrey ...15 G6
Voe Shet 61 c4

Waddesdon Bucks 14 E3
Waddington Lancs 33 G3
Waddington Lincs 30 F4
Wadebridge Cnwll 2 F4
Wadesmill Herts 15 K3
Wadhurst E Susx 10 E5
Wainfleet All Saints
Lincs 31 K4
Wakefield Wakefd 33 M5
Walberswick Suffk 25 L7
Walgherton Ches E 28 E5
Walkerburn Border 46 D6
Walkern Herts 16 B5
Walkington E R Yk 35 G3
Wallasey Wirral 32 C7
Wallingford Oxon 14 D5
Walls Shet 61 b5
Walsall Wsall 22 B1
Waltham NE Lin 35 J6
Waltham Abbey
Essex 16 C7
Waltham on the
Wolds Leics 30 E7
Walton Powys 21 G4
Walton Somset 12 F7
Walton-on-Thames
Surrey 15 H6
Walton-on-the-Naze
Essex 17 K5
Wanlockhead D & G 45 L6
Wansford C Pete 23 L1
Wanstrow Somset 13 H6
Wantage Oxon 14 B5
Warboys Cambs 24 A7

Warcop Cumb....37 K2
Wardlow Derbys....29 J3
Ware Herts....15 K3
Wareham Dorset....7 L3
Warenford Nthumb....47 L6
Wargrave Wokham....14 E6
Wark Nthumb....42 F4
Wark Nthumb....47 H6
Warkworth Nthumb....43 K2
Warlingham Surrey....10 C3
Warmington Warwks....22 E5
Warminster Wilts....13 J4
Warninglid W Susx....10 B5
Warrington Warrtn....32 F7
Warsash Hants....8 E5
Warslow Staffs....29 H4
Warton Lancs....32 D4
Warwick Warwks....22 D4
Wasbister Ork....65 b2
Wasdale Head Cumb....36 E3
Washingborough Lincs....30 F3
Washington Sundld....43 K6
Watchet Somset....5 J3
Watchgate Cumb....37 H4
Waterbeach Cambs....16 D2
Waterbeck D & G....42 A4
Waterhouses Staffs....29 H5
Waterlooville Hants....9 G5
Watermillock Cumb....37 G2
Watford Herts....15 H4
Watford Nhants....23 G4
Wath upon Dearne Rothm....34 B6
Watlington Oxon....14 E4
Watten Highld....65 H3
Watton Norfk....24 F5
Watton-at-Stone Herts....15 K2
Wearhead Dur....42 F7
Weasenham All Saints Norfk....24 F4
Weaverham Ches W....28 D3
Wedmore Somset....12 E6
Weedon Bec Nhants....23 G4
Week St Mary Cnwll....4 B7
Weem P & K....50 D2
Welborn Lincs....30 F4
Wellesbourne Warwks....22 D5
Wellingborough Nhants....23 J4
Wellington Somset....5 K5
Wellington Wrekin....28 D8
Wells Somset....12 F6
Wells-next-the-Sea Norfk....24 F2
Welney Norfk....24 C6
Welshampton Shrops....28 B6
Welshpool Powys....27 K8
Welton Nhants....23 G4
Welwyn Herts....15 J3
Welwyn Garden City Herts....15 J3
Wem Shrops....28 C6
Wembley Gt Lon....10 B5
Wembury Devon....3 L6
Wendover Bucks....14 F3
Wensley N York....38 B4
Wentbridge Wakefd....34 B5
Weobley Herefs....21 H5
Wereham Norfk....24 D5
West Auckland Dur....38 B2
West Bay Dorset....7 H3
West Bexington Dorset....7 H3
West Bilney Norfk....24 E4
West Bridgford Notts....30 C6
West Bromwich Sandw....22 B2
Westbury Shrops....28 B8
Westbury Wilts....13 J6
West Calder W Loth....46 A4
West Chiltington W Susx....9 K4
Westcott Surrey....9 L2
Westerham Kent....10 C3
West Felton Shrops....27 L7
Westfield E Susx....10 F6
Westgate-on-Sea Kent....11 L2
West Haddon Nhants....23 G3
Westhill Abers....55 L4
West Hoathly W Susx....10 C5
West Horsley Surrey....15 H8
West Huntspill Somset....12 D6
West Kilbride N Ayrs....44 F3
West Kirby Wirral....27 K2
West Lavington Wilts....13 K6
West Linton Border....46 C5

West Lulworth Dorset....7 L4
West Lynn Norfk....24 D4
West Malling Kent....10 E3
West Malvern Worcs....21 L5
West Meon Hants....9 G4
West Mersea Essex....17 H6
West Moors Dorset....8 B5
Westnewton Cumb....41 L7
West Newton Norfk....24 E3
Weston Herts....16 B4
Weston Staffs....29 G6
Westonbirt Gloucs....13 J3
Weston Heath Shrops....28 E7
Weston-on-the-Green Oxon....14 C3
Weston-sub-Edge Gloucs....22 C6
Weston-super-Mare N Som....12 D5
Weston-under-Redcastle Shrops....28 D6
West Pennard Somset....12 F7
West Pentire Cnwll....2 D5
West Rounton N York....38 D3
West Runton Norfk....25 J2
Westruther Border....47 G5
West Sandwick Shet....61 c3
Westward Ho! Devon....4 D4
West Wittering W Susx....9 H6
West Witton N York....38 A4
West Woodburn Nthumb....43 G3
Wetheral Cumb....42 C6
Wetherby Leeds....34 B3
Wetwang E R Yk....39 J7
Weybourne Norfk....25 H2
Weybridge Surrey....15 H7
Weyhill Hants....8 D2
Weymouth Dorset....7 J4
Whaley Bridge Derbys....29 G2
Whalley Lancs....33 G3
Whaplode Lincs....31 J7
Whaplode Drove Lincs....31 J7
Whauphill D & G....40 E6
Wheathampstead Herts....15 J3
Wheatley Oxon....14 D3
Wheddon Cross Somset....5 H4
Whepstead Suffk....17 G2
Wherwell Hants....8 E2
Whickham Gatesd....43 J5
Whiddon Down Devon....6 A3
Whimple Devon....6 D3
Whipsnade C Beds....15 G3
Whitburn W Loth....46 A4
Whitby N York....39 H3
Whitchurch Bucks....14 E2
Whitchurch Hants....8 E2
Whitchurch Herefs....21 H5
Whitchurch Shrops....28 C5
Whitebridge Highld....58 D7
Whitehaven Cumb....36 D2
Whitehill and Bordon Hants....9 H3
Whitehills Abers....60 D3
Whitehouse Ag & B....49 G6
Whitekirk E Loth....46 F2
Whitewell Lancs....32 F3
Whithorn D & G....40 E7
Whiting Bay N Ayrs....44 E5
Whitland Carmth....18 E5
Whitley Bay N Tyne....43 K5
Whitley Chapel Nthumb....43 G6
Whitminster Gloucs....13 H1
Whitstable Kent....11 J2
Whittington Shrops....27 L6
Whittlebury Nhants....23 H4
Whittlesey Cambs....24 A6
Whitton Powys....21 G4
Whitwell Derbys....30 B3
Whitwell Herts....15 J2
Wick Highld....65 J3
Wickford Essex....16 F4
Wickham Hants....8 F5
Wickham Market Suffk....17 K2
Wickwar S Glos....13 H3
Widdrington Nthumb....43 K3
Widecombe in the Moor Devon....6 A4
Widegates Cnwll....3 J5

Widemouth Bay Cnwll....4 B6
Widford Herts....16 C5
Widmerpool Notts....30 C6
Widnes Halton....28 C2
Wigan Wigan....32 E6
Wiggenhall St Germans Norfk....24 D4
Wigston Leics....23 G1
Wigton Cumb....42 A6
Wigtown D & G....40 E6
Wilberfoss E R Yk....34 D2
Wilby Nhants....23 J4
Willand Devon....5 J6
Willingham Cambs....24 B8
Williton Somset....5 J3
Wilmcote Warwks....22 C4
Wilmington Devon....6 F2
Wilmslow Ches E....28 F2
Wilsontown S Lans....46 A4
Wilstead Bed....23 L6
Wilton Wilts....13 L7
Wimbledon Gt Lon....15 J6
Wimblington Cambs....24 B6
Wimborne Minster Dorset....8 A5
Wincanton Somset....13 H7
Winchcombe Gloucs....22 B7
Winchelsea E Susx....11 G6
Winchester Hants....8 E3
Windermere Cumb....37 G4
Windsor W & M....15 G6
Wing Bucks....14 F2
Wingate Dur....43 L7
Wingham Kent....11 K3
Winkfield Br For....14 F6
Winkleigh Devon....6 F6
Winscombe N Som....12 E5
Winsford Ches W....28 D3
Winsford Somset....5 H4
Winsham Somset....7 G2
Winslow Bucks....23 H7
Winster Derbys....29 J4
Winterborne Monkton Dorset....7 J3
Winterborne Stickland Dorset....7 L2
Winterborne Whitechurch Dorset....7 L2
Winterborne Abbas Dorset....7 J3
Winterbourne Stoke Wilts....13 L7
Winteringham N Linc....34 F3
Winterslow Wilts....8 C3
Winterton N Linc....34 F5
Winwick Cambs....23 L3
Wirksworth Derbys....29 J4
Wisbech Cambs....31 K8
Wisborough Green W Susx....9 K3
Wishaw N Lans....45 L3
Witham Essex....16 F5
Witheridge Devon....5 G6
Withern Lincs....31 K2
Withernsea E R Yk....35 K4
Withington Gloucs....22 B8
Withington Herefs....21 J6
Witheyham E Susx....10 D5
Withypool Somset....5 H4
Witnesham Suffk....17 J3
Witney Oxon....14 B3
Wittersham Kent....11 G5
Witton le Wear Dur....43 J8
Wiveliscombe Somset....5 J4
Wivelsfield E Susx....10 C6
Wivenhoe Essex....17 H5
Wix Essex....17 J4
Woburn C Beds....23 K6
Woburn Sands M Keyn....23 J6
Woking Surrey....15 G7
Wokingham Wokham....14 F6
Wolf's Castle Pembks....18 C4
Wollaston Nhants....23 J4
Wollaston Shrops....27 L8
Wolsingham Dur....43 H7
Wolverhampton Wolves....21 M1
Wolvey Warwks....22 E2
Wolviston S on T....38 E2
Wombourne Staffs....21 M2
Wombwell Barns....34 B6
Wooburn Bucks....14 F5
Woodborough Notts....30 C6
Woodbridge Suffk....17 K3
Woodchurch Kent....11 G5
Woodford Gloucs....13 G2
Woodhall Spa Lincs....31 H4
Woodland Dur....38 B2
Woodstock Oxon....14 C3

Woofferton Shrops....21 J4
Wookey Hole Somset....12 F6
Wool Dorset....7 L3
Woolacombe Devon....4 D3
Wooler Nthumb....47 K6
Woolhampton W Berk....14 D6
Woolpit Suffk....17 H2
Woolwich Gt Lon....10 C1
Woore Shrops....28 E5
Wootton N Linc....35 G5
Wootton Oxon....14 B2
Wootton Bassett Wilts....13 L3
Wootton Courtenay Somset....5 H3
Wootton Wawen Warwks....22 C4
Worcester Worcs....21 M5
Workington Cumb....36 D1
Worksop Notts....30 C2
Worlingworth Suffk....17 K1
Wormit Fife....51 J4
Worplesdon Surrey....15 G7
Worthen Shrops....21 G1
Worthing W Susx....9 L5
Worth Matravers Dorset....7 M4
Wotton-under-Edge Gloucs....13 H3
Wragby Lincs....31 G3
Wrangaton Devon....6 A6
Wrangle Lincs....31 K5
Wrawby N Linc....35 G6
Wrelton N York....39 G5
Wrentham Suffk....25 L7
Wrestlingworth C Beds....16 B3
Wrexham Wrexhm....27 L5
Wrexham Industrial Estate Wrexhm....28 B5
Writtle Essex....16 E6
Wroughton Swindn....13 L4
Wroxall IoW....8 F7
Wroxeter Shrops....28 D8
Wroxham Norfk....25 K4
Wroxton Oxon....22 E6
Wyboston Bed....23 L5
Wye Kent....11 H4
Wylye Wilts....13 K7
Wymondham Leics....30 E7
Wymondham Norfk....25 H5

Y

Yarcombe Devon....6 F2
Yardley Gobion Nhants....23 H5
Yardley Hastings Nhants....23 J5
Yarm S on T....38 D3
Yarmouth IoW....8 D6
Yarrowford Border....46 E6
Yate S Glos....13 H3
Yateley Hants....14 F7
Yatton N Som....12 E5
Yatton Keynell Wilts....13 J4
Yaxley Cambs....23 M2
Yeadon Leeds....33 K3
Yealmpton Devon....3 L5
Yelverton Devon....3 L4
Yelverton Norfk....25 K5
Yeovil Somset....7 H1
Yeovilton Somset....12 F8
Yetts o'Muckhart Clacks....50 E6
Y Felinheli Gwynd....26 D3
Y Maerdy Conwy....27 J5
York C York....34 C2
Youlgreave Derbys....29 J4
Yoxall Staffs....29 H7
Yoxford Suffk....17 L1
Y Rhiw Gwynd....26 B6
Ysbyty Ystwyth Cerdgn....20 B3
Ystalyfera Neath....19 K5
Ystradgynlais Powys....19 K5
Ystrad Mynach Caerph....12 C2

Z

Zeals Wilts....13 H7
Zennor Cnwll....2 B6

This chart shows distances in miles between two towns along AA-recommended routes. Using motorways and other main roads this is normally the fastest route, though not necessarily the shortest.

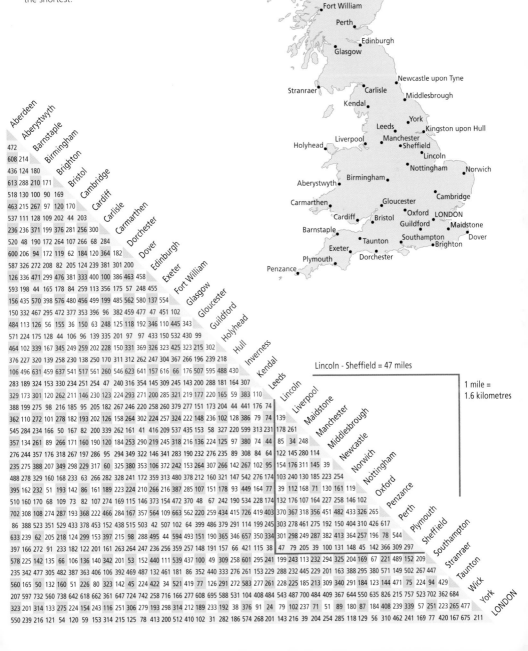

Lincoln - Sheffield = 47 miles

1 mile = 1.6 kilometres

Aberdeen																																										
472	Aberystwyth
608	214	Barnstaple
436	124	180	Birmingham
613	288	210	171	Brighton
518	130	100	90	169	Bristol
463	215	267	97	120	170	Cambridge
537	111	128	109	202	44	203	Cardiff
236	236	371	199	376	281	256	300	Carlisle
520	48	190	172	264	107	266	68	284	Carmarthen
600	206	94	172	119	62	184	120	364	182	Dorchester
587	326	272	208	82	205	124	239	381	301	200	Dover
126	336	471	299	476	381	333	400	100	386	463	458	Edinburgh
593	198	44	165	178	84	259	113	356	175	57	248	455	Exeter
156	435	570	398	576	480	456	499	199	485	562	580	137	554	Fort William
150	332	467	295	472	377	353	396	96	382	459	477	47	451	102	Glasgow
484	113	126	56	155	36	150	63	248	125	118	192	346	110	445	343	Gloucester
571	224	175	128	44	106	96	139	335	201	97	97	433	150	532	430	99	Guildford
464	102	339	167	345	249	259	202	228	150	331	369	326	323	425	323	215	302	Holyhead
376	227	320	139	258	230	138	250	170	311	312	262	247	304	367	266	196	239	218	Hull
106	496	631	459	637	541	517	561	260	546	623	641	157	616	66	176	507	595	488	430	Inverness
283	189	324	153	330	234	251	254	47	240	316	354	145	309	245	143	200	288	181	164	307	Kendal
329	173	301	120	262	211	146	230	123	224	293	271	200	285	321	219	177	220	165	59	383	110	Leeds
388	199	275	98	216	185	95	205	182	267	246	220	258	260	379	277	151	173	204	44	441	176	74	Lincoln
362	110	272	101	278	182	193	202	126	158	264	302	224	257	324	222	148	236	102	128	386	79	74	139	Liverpool
545	284	234	166	50	167	82	200	339	262	161	41	416	209	537	435	153	58	327	220	599	313	231	178	261	Maidstone
357	134	261	89	266	171	160	190	120	184	253	290	219	245	318	216	136	224	125	97	380	74	44	85	34	248	Manchester
276	244	357	176	318	267	197	286	95	294	349	322	146	341	283	190	232	276	235	89	308	84	64	122	146	280	114	Middlesbrough
235	275	388	207	349	298	229	317	60	325	380	353	106	372	242	153	264	307	266	142	267	102	95	154	176	311	145	39	Newcastle
488	278	329	160	168	233	63	266	282	328	241	172	359	313	480	378	212	160	321	147	542	276	174	103	240	130	185	223	254	Norwich
395	162	232	51	193	142	86	161	189	223	224	210	266	216	387	285	107	151	178	93	449	164	77	39	112	168	71	130	161	119	Nottingham
510	160	170	68	109	73	82	107	274	169	115	146	373	154	472	370	48	67	242	190	534	228	174	132	176	107	164	227	258	146	102	Oxford
702	308	108	274	287	193	368	222	466	284	167	357	564	109	663	562	220	259	434	415	726	419	403	370	367	318	356	451	482	433	326	265	Penzance
86	388	523	351	529	433	378	453	152	438	515	503	42	507	102	64	399	486	379	311	114	199	245	303	278	461	275	192	150	404	310	426	617	Perth
633	239	62	205	218	124	299	153	397	215	98	288	495	44	594	493	151	190	365	346	657	350	334	301	298	249	287	382	413	364	257	196	78	544	Plymouth
397	166	272	91	233	182	122	201	161	263	264	247	236	256	359	257	148	191	157	66	421	115	38	47	79	205	39	100	131	148	45	142	366	309	297	Sheffield
578	225	142	135	66	106	136	140	342	201	53	152	440	111	539	437	100	49	309	258	601	295	241	199	243	113	232	294	325	204	169	67	221	489	152	209	Southampton
235	342	477	305	482	387	363	406	106	392	469	487	132	461	181	86	352	440	333	276	261	153	229	288	232	445	229	201	163	388	295	380	571	149	502	267	447	Stranraer
560	165	50	132	160	51	226	80	323	142	45	224	422	34	521	419	77	126	291	272	583	277	261	228	225	185	213	309	340	291	184	123	144	471	75	224	94	429	Taunton
207	597	732	560	738	642	618	662	361	647	724	742	258	716	166	277	608	695	588	531	104	408	484	543	487	700	484	409	367	644	550	635	826	215	757	523	702	362	684	Wick
323	201	314	133	275	224	154	243	116	251	306	279	193	298	314	212	189	233	192	38	376	91	24	79	102	237	71	51	89	180	87	184	408	239	339	57	251	223	265	477	York
505	239	216	121	54	120	59	153	314	215	125	78	413	200	512	410	102	31	282	186	574	268	201	143	216	39	204	254	285	118	129	56	310	462	241	169	77	420	167	675	211	LONDON

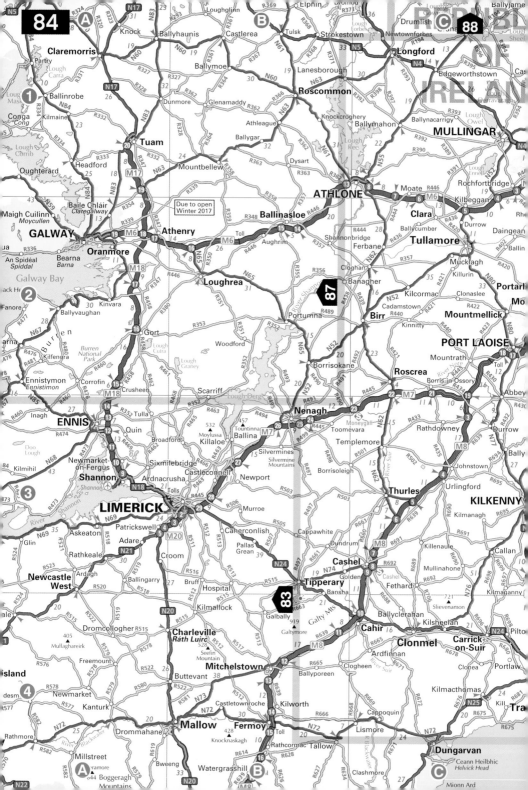

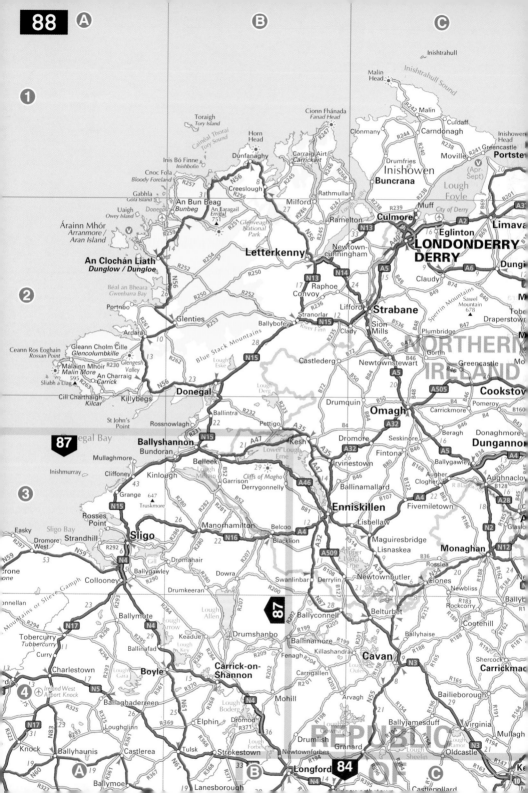

This chart shows distances, in both miles and kilometres, between two towns along AA-recommended routes. Using motorways and other main roads this is normally the fastest route, though not always the shortest.

For example, the distance between Clifden and Mullingar is |206| kilometres or |128| miles (8 kilometres is approximately 5 miles).

To reflect the distances shown on road signs, distances shown on the road maps in this atlas are in miles in Northern Ireland and kilometres in the Republic of Ireland.

Distances in miles

```
Antrim        42 150 153 322  18 165 169  99 221  38 332 105  93  38 114  60 106 221  75 203 150 255 190 301  22 235  54 119  53 166 143 208 116 227 296 153 215 193 143
Armagh           99 127 290  40 134 143  48 194  60 239 294  74  52  81  29  94 170  47 150 124 204 158 269  63 203  70  91  36 134 101 176  90 195 263 121 183 162 111
Athlone              83 181 149  72  81  51 101 157 130 164 114 150  76 106 148  71  81  53  62 105  78 139 171  73 133  29 101  48  20 126  34  74  86 134  24 110 117 106
Ballina                 231 160 153  24 101  75 150 184 216  76 171 147 140 112 104  79  70  30 138 160 191 183 124 121 100 103 130  63 208  37 149 186 106 192 199 177
Bantry                      313 163 217 244 218 353  52  84 286 305 209 262 319 132 275 170 216 107 140  43 335 110 326 201 293 157 292 170 246 116  64 176 126 162 205
Belfast           68            156 176  97 228  87 262 317 106  22 104  52 201 125 250 190 157 281 181 292  23 226  71 110 164 157 142 199 124 217 286 144 206 162 134
Carlow           242 159        152 117 171 196 111 185 184 148  52 104 219 118 147 134 150  24 160 178  94 196  75  68  24  91  55 145  71 155  44  49  46  56
Castlebar        246 204 133    104  52 167 168 200  93 188 146 157 128  88  95  47  29 122 159  51 199 127 129  89 153 132 170 144  59  26  53 132 170 110 149 157 103
Cavan            518 467 292 374 151 116 192 213  68 108  71  51 103 122  30 103  85 156 142 188 119 122  82  44  49  88  53 168  62 149 182  68 167 153 103
Clifden           29  65 239 258 504 218 168 201 144 239 176 206 179  89 146  48  80 122 158 176 250 108 188 128 170 147  96 225 104 134 170 124 188 216 206
Coleraine        266 215 116 247 262 251 308 359  76  75 152  98  84 229  85 198 149 263 228 339  47 273  32 152  64 204 149 246 115 265 334 175 253 231 181
Cork             272 230 130  39 349 284 245  95 238 253 157 209 273  85 222 122 168 116  89  55 283  62 274 149 241 104 171 118 198  63  75 124  75 110 153
Daingean         159  78  82 159 392 156 188 167 269 309 213 265 304 116 243 153 199  76 173  41 339  39 294 122 127 147 111  35 158  37 126  73 194 190 246
Donegal          355 313 162 121 351 367 276  83 243 127 147 111  35 158  37 126  73 194 190 246 115 177  46 121  41 159  91 238  40 202 242 139 222 229 180
Downpatrick       61  97 253 242 568  87 316 268 170 351 107  54 137 222  92 202 168 273 173 284  44 218  92 102  80 149 153 191 135 210 278 136 198 176 126
Dublin           435  59 209 296  84 421 179 270 309 271 496  52 169 147 100 128 127 178  78 188 126 122 144  50 111  53  96  97 129 114 183  63 103  82  31
Dundalk          169 473 264 348 135 510 298 322 342 323 575 153 121 198  63 158 137 229 129 240  74 174  94  58  62 105  99 148 104 166 235  93 155 133  82
An Clochán Liath 150 119 183 180 460 171 296 149 109 231 123 383 433 192  77 158 109 226 244 205 121 272  24 206 101 173  93  77 144 118  48  86  96 103 136 173
Ennis             61  83 241 276 491  35 238 302 174 385 121 407 497 204 134  75 186 171 217 103 152  52  75  25 118  65 198 213 179 213  98 196 183 132
Enniskillen      183 131 123 237 337 168  84 235 114 283 244 253 343 237 173  53  75 111 129 232  61 167  80 152 100  48 178  83  86 123  76 140 169 158
Galway            97  46 171 225 421  83 168 252  82 331 158 337 427 178  87  83 121 140 174 180 106 117  80  99 109  42 188  34 132 168  86 172 179 157
Ireland West      170 151 239 180 513 201 353 206 165 288 135 439 490  56 222 272 194 137  64 303  55 239 134 206 125 110 175 151  80  45 130 134 167 204
Kilkee           356 274 115 168 213 402 190 142 197 143 369 136 186 254 357 236 319 309 127 203  81 221  76 188  98  62 152  53 142  51  31  54  87
Kilkenny         120  76 131 117 442 130 236 153  49 235 136 358 391  59 148 161 101 124 248 314  68 270 167 233 165 160 204  91  21 141 119 152 216
Killarney        326 243  85 113 274 306 199  76 166  78 319 196 247 202 325 207 255 254  67 214 248  75 132  74 179 163 221 146 240 309 166 228 206 156
Larne            241 199 100  48 348 253 215  46 137 128 239 270 321 118 271 205 220 175 141 121  85 205 103 172  71  99 120 137  25  63  76  79 112 151
Limerick         410 328 169 222 172 452 241 196 251 197 423 186 122 313 439 286 369 363  52 299 121 195 126  33 170 117 240  84 231 264 150 247 226 175
Londonderry      306 255 128 226 226 292  39 256 229 255 367 143 278 306 279 125 208 393 169 276 178 226 220  93  45 128  81 106 162  25 107 119  79
Mullingar        484 433 224 308  70 470 257 282 302 283 545  88  6 456 546 186  71 202 119 203 438 596 394 488 327 506 137  89 208  66 192 232 113 164 169 158
Omagh             35 101 275 294 539  37 287 320 192 402  76 456 546 186  71 202 119 203 438 596 394 488 327 506  68  78 122  62 130  21  63  70  80
Port Laoise      378 327 118 199 177 364 152 173 196 174 439  99 150 285 351 197 281 340  38 245  98 171  88 131 110 399 145  55 107 158  43 130 137 126
Roscommon         87 113 214 194 525 114 316 220 132 302  51 441 474  74 148 231 152  83 331  83 269 189 384 356 434 120 330 199  96 176  98  44   9  68
Rosslare         191 147  46 161 323 177 121 159  71 206 244 240 309 195 164  80  93 237 162 120 129 129 216 122 269 212 165 203 162 199  98 184 191 158
Sligo             86  58 162 165 472 110 264 191  79 274 103 389 440  66 128 179 100 94 278  40 245 160 332 303 381 119 277  53 150  85  81  54  81  54  87
Tipperary        267 215  77 209 252 252  39 207 142 237 328 168 259 256 239  86 169 307 150 190 161 176 204 278  65  72 221  230 162  32 101 325 228 147  98  85 154 239 276 303 147 246 155 159 208 124 104  70  68 177 158 264 263 159 188  72 143 109
Tralee           335 284 202 334 273 321  88 332 271 362 396 190 333 383 308 156 238 435 232 318 286 302 282 100 258 356 193 387 206 334 126 234
Tullamore        187 145 119  59 396 199 234  85 100 168 185 319 371  65 217 207 167 121 190  67 134  54 243 245 329 235 221 135 130 107 196  88 321  83  89  93
Waterford        365 314 139 240 186 350 114 213 239 215 426 102 187 325 338 184 267 381  78  42 138 212 129  85 146 386  40 371 170 319  99 172 154 261  37  80
Wexford          476 424 215 299 103 461 273 278 293 278 448 295 378 441 138 342 198 271  22  28 497 102 425 288 253 283 321 137  53
Wicklow          246 195  39 170 283 232  71 168 109 199 281 200 261 223 219 101 149 275 155 132 138 209  82  52 138 209  42 227 123 241  40 189  33  70 158 158 130 218
                 346 295 177 309 203 332  79 307 269 302 407 120 266 357 319 165 249 433 165 342 225 277 216  50 192 367 127 398 173 345 101 209  71 296  87 216 133
                 311 260 188 320 260 260  74 318 245 348 372 177 322 369 284 132 214 411 219 294 272 288 269  87 245 332 181 363 192 310 112 220  15 308 141 270 144  59
                 230 178 171 285 330 215  90 282 166 331 291 246 388 289 202  50 132 330 279 213 255 252 329 140 347 251 243 261 127 229 129 202 110 255 227 338 149 128  86
```

Distances in kilometres

This index lists places appearing in the main-map section of the atlas in alphabetical order. The reference following each name gives the atlas page number and grid reference of the square in which the place appears. The map shows government districts (Northern Ireland), counties and administrative districts, together with a list of the abbreviated name forms used in the index.

Northern Ireland Districts

A & ND	**Ards and North Down**
A & N	**Antrim & Newtownabbey**
AB & C	**Armagh City, Banbridge & Craigavon**
Belfst	**Belfast (1)**
CC & G	**Causeway Coast & Glens**
D & S	**Derry City & Strabane**
E Antr	**Mid & East Antrim**
F & O	**Fermanagh & Omagh**
L & C	**Lisburn & Castlereagh City**
M Ulst	**Mid Ulster**
NM & D	**Newry, Mourne and Down**

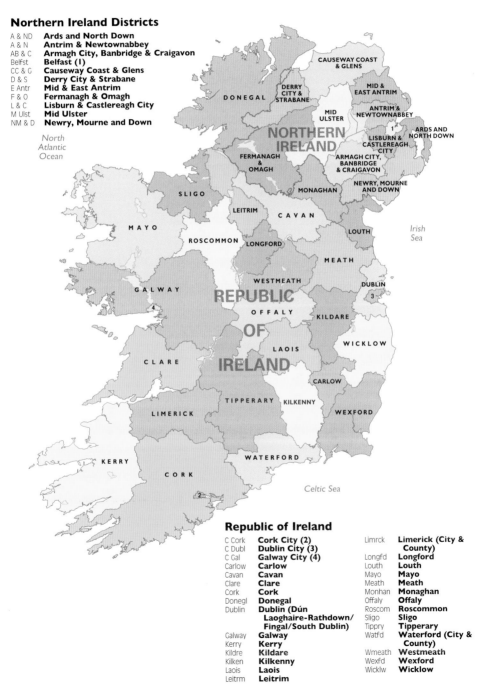

Republic of Ireland

C Cork	**Cork City (2)**		Limrck	**Limerick (City & County)**
C Dubl	**Dublin City (3)**			
C Gal	**Galway City (4)**		Longfd	**Longford**
Carlow	**Carlow**		Louth	**Louth**
Cavan	**Cavan**		Mayo	**Mayo**
Clare	**Clare**		Meath	**Meath**
Cork	**Cork**		Monhan	**Monaghan**
Donegl	**Donegal**		Offaly	**Offaly**
Dublin	**Dublin (Dún Laoghaire-Rathdown/ Fingal/South Dublin)**		Roscom	**Roscommon**
			Sligo	**Sligo**
			Tippry	**Tipperary**
Galway	**Galway**		Watfd	**Waterford (City & County)**
Kerry	**Kerry**			
Kildre	**Kildare**		Wmeath	**Westmeath**
Kilken	**Kilkenny**		Wexfd	**Wexford**
Laois	**Laois**		Wicklw	**Wicklow**
Leitrm	**Leitrim**			

A

Abbeydorney Kerry 82 C2
Abbeyfeale Limrck 82 C2
Abbeyleix Laois 84 C2
Adare Limrck 83 D2
Adrigole Cork 82 C3
Aghalee L & C 89 D3
Ahoghill E Antr 89 D2
Allenwood Kildre 85 D2
Allihies Cork 82 B3
An Bun Beag
   Donegl 88 B2
An Charraig Donegl 88 A2
An Cheathrú Rua
   Galway 86 B3
An Clochán Liath
   Donegl 88 A2
An Coireán Kerry 82 B3
An Daingean Kerry 82 B2
Annahilt L & C 89 E3
Annalong NM & D 89 E4
Annascaul Kerry 82 B2
An Spidéal Galway 86 C3
Antrim A & N 89 D2
Ardagh Limrck 83 D2
Ardara Donegl 88 A2
Ardee Louth 89 D4
Ardfert Kerry 82 C2
Ardfinnan Tippry 84 C4
Ardglass NM & D 89 E3
Ardmore Watfd 83 E3
Ardnacrusha Clare 83 D1
Arklow Wicklw 85 E3
Armagh AB & C 89 D3
Armoy CC & G 89 D1
Arvagh Cavan 88 B4
Ashbourne Meath 85 E1
Ashford Wicklw 85 E2
Askeaton Limrck 83 D1
Athboy Meath 85 D1
Athenry Galway 87 D3
Athleague Roscom 87 D3
Athlone Wmeath 84 C1
Athy Kildre 85 D2
Augher M Ulst 88 C3
Aughnacloy M Ulst 88 C3
Aughrim Galway 87 D3
Aughrim Wicklw 85 E3
Avoca Wicklw 85 E3

B

Bagenalstown
   Carlow 85 D3
Baile an
   Fheirtéaraigh
   Kerry 82 B2
Baile Chláir Galway 86 C3
Baile Mhic Íre Cork 82 C3
Bailieborough
   Cavan 88 C4
Balbriggan Dublin 85 E1
Ballaghaderreen
   Roscom 87 D2
Ballina Mayo 86 C2
Ballina Tippry 83 D1
Ballinafad Sligo 87 D2
Ballinagar Offaly 84 C2
Ballinamallard F & O 88 B3
Ballinamore Leitrm 87 E2
Ballinasloe Galway 87 D3
Ballincollig Cork 83 D3
Ballindaggan Wexfd 85 D3

Ballingarry Limrck 83 D2
Ballingeary Cork 82 C3
Ballinrobe Mayo 86 C3
Ballinspittle Cork 83 D3
Ballivor Meath 85 D1
Ballybay Monhan 88 C4
Ballybofey Donegl 88 B2
Ballybunion Kerry 82 C2
Ballycanew Wexfd 85 E3
Ballycarry E Antr 89 E2
Ballycastle CC & G 89 D1
Ballycastle Mayo 86 C1
Ballyclare A & N 89 E2
Ballyclerahan Tippry 84 C4
Ballyconneely
   Galway 86 B3
Ballyconnell Cavan 88 B4
Ballycotton Cork 83 E3
Ballycumber Offaly 84 C2
Ballydehob Cork 82 C4
Ballydesmond Cork 82 C2
Ballyferriter Kerry 82 B2
Ballygally E Antr 89 E2
Ballygar Galway 87 D3
Ballygawley M Ulst 88 C3
Ballygawley Sligo 87 D1
Ballygowan A & ND 89 E3
Ballyhack Wexfd 85 D4
Ballyhaise Cavan 88 C4
Ballyhalbert A & ND 89 E3
Ballyhaunis Mayo 87 D2
Ballyheige Kerry 82 B2
Ballyjamesduff
   Cavan 88 C4
Ballylongford Kerry 82 C2
Ballymahon Longfd 84 C1
Ballymakeery Cork 82 C3
Ballymena E Antr 89 D2
Ballymoe Galway 87 D2
Ballymoney CC & G 89 D2
Ballymore Eustace
   Kildre 85 D2
Ballymote Sligo 87 D2
Ballynacarrigy
   Wmeath 84 C1
Ballynahinch
   NM & D 89 E3
Ballynure A & N 89 E2
Ballyporeen Tippry 84 B4
Ballyragget Kilken 84 C3
Ballyshannon
   Donegl 87 D1
Ballyvaughan Clare 86 C4
Ballywalter A & ND 89 E3
Balrothery Dublin 85 E1
Baltimore Cork 82 C4
Baltinglass Wicklw 85 D2
Banagher Offaly 84 C2
Banbridge AB & C 89 D3
Bandon Cork 83 D3
Bangor A & ND 89 E2
Bangor Erris Mayo 86 B2
Bansha Tippry 84 B3
Bantry Cork 82 C3
Barna Galway 86 C3
Béal an Mhuirthead
   Mayo 86 B1
Béal Átha an
   Ghaorthaidh
   Cork 82 C3
Bearna Galway 86 C3
Belcoo F & O 87 E1
Belfast Belfst 89 E3
Belgooly Cork 83 D3
Bellaghy M Ulst 89 D2

Belleek F & O 87 D1
Belmullet Mayo 86 B1
Belturbet Cavan 88 C4
Benburb M Ulst 89 D3
Beragh F & O 88 C3
Bessbrook NM & D 89 D3
Birr Offaly 84 C2
Blacklion Cavan 87 E1
Blackwater Wexfd 85 E3
Blarney Cork 83 D3
Blessington Wicklw 85 D2
Borris Carlow 85 D3
Borris-in-Ossory
   Laois 84 C2
Borrisokane Tippry 87 D4
Borrisoleigh Tippry 84 C3
Boyle Roscom 87 D2
Bray Wicklw 85 E2
Bridgetown Wexfd 85 D4
Brittas Dublin 85 E2
Broadford Clare 83 D1
Broughshane E Antr 89 D2
Bruff Limrck 83 D2
Bunbeg Donegl 88 B2
Bunclody Wexfd 85 D3
Buncrana Donegl 88 C1
Bundoran Donegl 87 D1
Bunnyconnellan
   Mayo 86 C2
Bushmills CC & G 89 D1
Buttevant Cork 83 D2
Bweeng Cork 83 D3

C

Cadamstown Offaly 84 C2
Caherconlish Limrck 83 D1
Caherdaniel Kerry 82 B3
Cahersiveen Kerry 82 B3
Cahir Tippry 84 C4
Caledon M Ulst 88 C3
Callan Kilken 84 C3
Camp Kerry 82 B2
Carndonagh Donegl 88 C1
Cappawhite Tippry 83 E1
Cappoquin Watfd 84 C4
Carlingford Louth 89 D4
Carlow Carlow 85 D3
Carna Galway 86 B3
Carnew Wicklw 85 E3
Carnlough E Antr 89 E2
Carragh Kildre 85 D2
Carraig Airt Donegl 88 B1
Carraroe Galway 86 B3
Carrick Donegl 88 A2
Carrickart Donegl 88 B1
Carrickfergus E Antr 89 E2
Carrickmacross
   Monhan 89 D4
Carrickmore F & O 88 C3
Carrick-on-
   Shannon Leitrm 87 D2
Carrick-on-Suir
   Tippry 84 C4
Carrigaline Cork 83 D3
Carrigallen Leitrm 88 B4
Carrigtwohill Cork 83 E3
Carryduff L & C 89 E3
Cashel Tippry 84 C3
Castlebar Mayo 86 C2
Castlebellingham
   Louth 89 D4
Castleblayney
   Monhan 89 D4
Castlebridge Wexfd 85 E4

Castlecomer Kilken 85 D3
Castleconnell Limrck 83 D1
Castlederg D & S 88 B2
Castledermot Kildre 85 D2
Castlegregory Kerry 82 B2
Castleisland Kerry 82 C2
Castlemaine Kerry 82 C2
Castlemartyr Cork 83 E3
Castlepollard
   Wmeath 84 C1
Castlerea Roscom 87 D2
Castlerock CC & G 88 C1
Castletownbere
   Cork 82 B3
Castletownroche
   Cork 83 D2
Castletownshend
   Cork 82 C4
Castlewellan
   NM & D 89 E3
Cathair Dónall
   Kerry 82 B3
Cavan Cavan 88 C4
Celbridge Kildre 85 D2
Charlestown Mayo 86 C2
Charleville Cork 83 D2
Cill Charthaigh
   Donegl 88 A2
Clady D & S 88 C2
Clane Kildre 85 D2
Clara Offaly 84 C2
Claregalway
   Galway 86 C3
Claremorris Mayo 86 C2
Clashmore Watfd 83 E3
Claudy D & S 88 C2
Cleggan Galway 86 B3
Clifden Galway 86 B3
Cliffoney Sligo 87 D1
Cloghan Offaly 84 C2
Clogheen Tippry 84 B4
Clogher M Ulst 88 C3
Clogherhead Louth 89 D4
Clogh Mills CC & G 89 D2
Clonakilty Cork 83 D4
Clonaslee Laois 84 C2
Clondalkin Dublin 85 E2
Clonea Watfd 84 C4
Clones Monhan 88 C3
Clonmany Donegl 88 C1
Clonmel Tippry 84 C4
Cloyne Cork 83 E3
Coachford Cork 83 D3
Coagh M Ulst 89 D2
Coalisland M Ulst 89 D3
Cobh Cork 83 E3
Coleraine CC & G 89 D1
Collon Louth 89 D4
Collooney Sligo 87 D1
Comber A & ND 89 E3
Cong Mayo 86 C3
Conga Mayo 86 C3
Convoy Donegl 88 B2
Cookstown M Ulst 89 D2
Cootehill Cavan 88 C4
Cork C Cork 83 D3
Corrofin Clare 86 C4
Courtown Wexfd 85 E3
Craigavon AB & C 89 D3
Creeslough Donegl 88 B1
Crookhaven Cork 82 C4
Crookstown Cork 83 D3
Croom Limrck 83 D2
Crosshaven Cork 83 E3
Crossmaglen
   NM & D 89 D4

Crossmolina Mayo 86 C2
Crumlin A & N 89 D2
Crusheen Clare 86 C4
Culdaff Donegl............ 88 C1
Cullybackey E Antr 89 D2
Culmore D & S............. 88 C2
Curry Sligo 87 D2
Cushendall CC & G...... 89 D1
Cushendun CC & G...... 89 D1

D

Daingean Offaly........... 84 C2
Daingean Uí Chúis
  Kerry 82 B2
Delvin Wmeath 85 D1
Derrinturn Kildre 85 D2
Derry D & S................. 88 C2
Derrygonnelly
  F & O 87 E1
Derrylin F & O 88 B3
Dingle Kerry 82 B2
Doagh A & N 89 D2
Donabate Dublin 85 E1
Donaghadee
  A & ND 89 E2
Donaghmore
  M Ulst..................... 88 C3
Donaghmore
  Meath..................... 85 D1
Donegal Donegl......... 88 B2
Doolin Clare................ 86 C4
Doonbeg Clare............ 82 C1
Downpatrick
  NM & D................... 89 E3
Dowra Leitrm............. 87 E1
Draperstown
  M Ulst..................... 89 D2
Drimoleague Cork....... 82 C3
Drogheda Louth.......... 85 E1
Droichead Nua
  Kildre 85 D2
Dromahair Leitrm 87 D1
Dromara L & C 89 E3
Dromcollogher
  Limrck.................... 83 D2
Dromiskin Louth 89 D4
Drommahane Cork...... 83 D3
Dromod Leitrm........... 87 E2
Dromore AB & C 89 D3
Dromore F & O 88 C3
Dromore West
  Sligo....................... 86 C1
Drumaness NM & D..... 89 E3
Drumfries Donegl....... 88 C1
Drumkeeran Leitrm..... 87 D1
Drumlish Longfd......... 88 B4
Drumquin F & O 88 C3
Drumshanbo
  Leitrm 87 E2
Dublin C Dubl 85 E2
Duleek Meath.............. 85 E1
Dunboyne Meath 85 D1
Dundalk Louth............. 89 D4
Dundonald L & C 89 E3
Dundrum Tippry 84 B3
Dunfanaghy Donegl.... 88 B1
Dungannon M Ulst...... 89 D3
Dungarvan Watfd 83 F3
Dungiven CC & G........ 88 C2
Dunglow Donegl......... 88 A2
Dún Laoghaire
  Dublin 85 E2
Dunlavin Wicklw 85 D2
Dunleer Louth............. 89 D4

Dunloy CC & G............ 89 D2
Dunmanway Cork....... 82 C3
Dunmore Galway 87 D3
Dunmore East
  Watfd 85 D4
Dunshaughlin
  Meath..................... 85 D1
Durrow Laois.............. 84 C3
Durrow Offaly 84 C2
Durrus Cork................ 82 C4
Dysart Roscom 87 D3

E

Easky Sligo 86 C1
Edenderry Offaly 85 D2
Edgeworthstown
  Longfd.................... 84 C1
Eglinton D & S............ 88 C2
Elphin Roscom 87 D2
Enfield Meath 85 D1
Ennis Clare................. 83 D1
Enniscorthy
  Wexfd 85 D3
Enniscrone Sligo 86 C1
Enniskean Cork 83 D3
Enniskillen F & O 88 B3
Ennistymon Clare 86 C4

F

Fanore Clare 86 C4
Farranfore Kerry 82 C2
Fenagh Leitrm 87 E2
Ferbane Offaly............ 84 C2
Fermoy Cork............... 83 E2
Ferns Wexfd............... 85 E3
Fethard Tippry............ 84 C3
Fethard Wexfd............ 85 D4
Fintona F & O.............. 88 C3
Fivemiletown
  M Ulst..................... 88 C3
Foxford Mayo.............. 86 C2
Freemount Cork 83 D2

G

Galbally Limrck 83 E2
Galway C Gal 86 C3
Garrison F & O 87 D1
Garvagh CC & G 89 D2
Gilford AB & C 89 D3
Glaslough Monhan 88 C3
Gleann Cholm Cille
  Donegl 88 A2
Glenamaddy
  Galway 87 D3
Glenarm E Antr 89 E2
Glenavy L & C 89 D3
Glenbeigh Kerry 82 B3
Glencolumbkille
  Donegl 88 A2
Glengarriff Cork 82 C3
Glenties Donegl.......... 88 B2
Glin Limrck 82 C2
Golden Tippry............. 84 B3
Goresbridge Kilken..... 85 D3
Gorey Wexfd 85 E3
Gort Galway 86 C4
Gortin F & O................ 88 C2
Gowran Kilken............ 85 D3
Graiguenamanagh
  Kilken 85 D3

Granard Longfd........... 88 C4
Grange Sligo............... 87 D1
Greencastle Donegl.... 88 C1
Greencastle F & O 88 C2
Greenore Louth 89 D4
Greyabbey A & ND 89 E3
Greystones Wicklw..... 85 E2
Gulladuff M Ulst......... 89 D2

H

Hacketstown
  Carlow.................... 85 D3
Headford Galway 86 C3
Hilltown NM & D......... 89 D3
Holywood A & ND 89 E2
Hospital Limrck........... 83 D2
Howth Dublin.............. 85 E1

I

Inagh Clare 82 C1
Inch Kerry 82 B2
Inishcrone Sligo.......... 86 C1
Innishannon Cork 83 D3
Irvinestown F & O....... 88 B3

J

Johnstown Kilken........ 84 C3

K

Kanturk Cork 83 D2
Keadue Roscom 87 D2
Keady AB & C 89 D3
Kealkill Cork 82 C3
Keel Mayo................... 86 B2
Kells Meath................. 85 D1
Kenmare Kerry 82 C3
Kesh F & O 88 B3
Kilbeggan Wmeath 84 C2
Kilcar Donegl............. 88 A2
Kilcock Meath 85 D1
Kilcoole Wicklw 85 E2
Kilcormac Offaly 84 C2
Kilcullen Kildre 85 D2
Kildare Kildre.............. 85 D2
Kilfenora Clare............ 86 C4
Kilgarvan Kerry........... 82 C3
Kilkee Clare 82 C1
Kilkeel NM & D 89 E4
Kilkenny Kilken 84 C3
Kill Kildre 85 D2
Kill Watfd 84 C4
Killala Mayo 86 C1
Killaloe Clare 83 D1
Killarney Kerry 82 C3
Killashandra Cavan 88 C4
Killenaule Tippry 84 C3
Killorglin Kerry 82 C2
Killucan Wmeath 85 D1
Killurin Offaly 84 C2
Killybegs Donegl........ 88 A2
Killyleagh NM & D 89 E3
Kilmacanogue
  Wicklw 85 E2
Kilmacthomas
  Watfd 84 C4
Kilmaganny Kilken 84 C3
Kilmaine Mayo 86 C3
Kilmallock Limrck 83 D2

Kilmanagh Kilken 84 C3
Kilmihil Clare 82 C1
Kilmore Quay
  Wexfd 85 D4
Kilmuckridge
  Wexfd 85 E3
Kilpedder Wicklw 85 E2
Kilrea CC & G 89 D2
Kilrush Clare............... 82 C1
Kilsheelan Tippry 84 C4
Kiltimagh Mayo 86 C2
Kilworth Cork 83 E2
Kingscourt Cavan 89 D4
Kinlough Leitrm.......... 87 D1
Kinnegad Meath 85 D1
Kinnitty Offaly............ 84 C2
Kinsale Cork 83 D3
Kinvara Galway 86 C4
Kircubbin A & ND 89 E3
Knock Mayo................ 86 C2
Knockcroghery
  Roscom.................... 87 D3

L

Lanesborough
  Longfd 84 B1
Laragh Wicklw 85 E2
Larne E Antr 89 E2
Lauragh Kerry 82 C3
Leap Cork 82 C4
Leenaun Galway.......... 86 B3
Leighlinbridge
  Carlow.................... 85 D3
Leixlip Kildre 85 D2
Letterfrack
  Galway 86 B3
Letterkenny
  Donegl 88 B2
Lifford Donegl............ 88 C2
Limavady CC & G 88 C2
Limerick Limrck 83 D1
Lisbellaw F & O 88 C3
Lisburn L & C 89 D3
Lisdoonvarna Clare..... 86 C4
Lismore Watfd 84 C4
Lisnaskea F & O 88 C3
Listowel Kerry............. 82 C2
Londonderry
  D & S 88 C2
Longford Longfd......... 84 C1
Longwood Meath........ 85 D1
Loughbrickland
  AB & C 89 D3
Loughglinn
  Roscom.................... 87 D2
Loughrea Galway 87 D4
Louisburgh Mayo 86 B2
Lucan Dublin 85 E2
Lurgan AB & C 89 D3
Lusk Dublin 85 E1

M

Macroom Cork............ 83 D3
Maghera M Ulst 89 D2
Magherafelt M Ulst...... 89 D2
Maguiresbridge
  F & O 88 C3
Maigh Cuilinn
  Galway 86 C3
Malahide Dublin 85 E1
Málainn Mhóir
  Donegl 88 A2

Malin Donegl 88 C1
Malin More Donegl 88 A2
Mallow Cork 83 D2
Manorhamilton
   Leitrm 87 D1
Markethill AB & C 89 D3
Maynooth Kildre 85 D1
Mayobridge
   NM & D 89 D3
Midleton Cork 83 E3
Milford Donegl 88 B2
Millstreet Cork 83 D3
Miltown Malbay
   Clare 82 C1
Mitchelstown
   Cork 83 E2
Moate Wmeath 84 C1
Mohill Leitrm 87 E2
Monaghan Monhan 88 C3
Monasterevin
   Kildre......................... 85 D2
Moneymore M Ulst 89 D2
Mooncoin Kilken 84 C4
Mountbellew
   Galway 87 D3
Mountmellick
   Laois 84 C2
Mountrath Laois 84 C2
Moville Donegl 88 C1
Moy M Ulst 89 D3
Moycullen Galway........ 86 C3
Mucklagh Offaly 84 C2
Muff Donegl 88 C2
Muine Bheag
   Carlow 85 D3
Mullagh Cavan 88 C4
Mullaghmore Sligo 87 D1
Mullinahone Tippry 84 C3
Mullingar Wmeath 84 C1
Mulranny Mayo 86 B2
Murrisk Mayo 86 B2
Murroe Limrck 83 D1

N

Naas Kildre.................. 85 D2
Naul Dublin.................. 85 E1
Navan Meath 85 D1
Nenagh Tippry 83 E1
Newbawn Wexfd 85 D4
Newbliss Monhan........ 88 C3
Newbridge Kildre 85 D2
Newcastle NM & D 89 E3
Newcastle Wicklw 85 E2
Newcastle West
   Limrck 83 D2
Newmarket Cork 83 D2
Newmarket-on-
   Fergus Clare 83 D1
Newport Mayo............ 86 B2
Newport Tippry 83 D1
New Ross Wexfd 85 D4
Newry NM & D 89 D3
Newtownabbey
   A & N......................... 89 E2
Newtownards
   A & ND 89 E3
Newtownbutler
   F & O 88 C3
Newtowncunningham
   Donegl.....................88 C2
Newtownforbes
   Longfd 84 C1
Newtownhamilton
   NM & D 89 D3

Newtownmountkennedy
   Wicklw 85 E2
Newtownstewart
   D & S 88 C2

O

Oldcastle Meath 88 C4
Omagh F & O 88 C3
Oranmore Galway........ 86 C3
Oughterard Galway 86 C3

P

Pallas Green Limrck 83 E2
Partry Mayo 86 C2
Passage East Watfd...... 85 D2
Passage West Cork 83 E3
Patrickswell Limrck 83 D1
Pettigo Donegl 88 B3
Piltown Kilken.............. 84 C4
Plumbridge D & S........ 88 C2
Pomeroy M Ulst........... 88 C3
Portadown AB & C...... 89 D3
Portaferry A & ND........ 89 E3
Portarlington Laois...... 85 D2
Portavogie A & ND...... 89 E3
Portglenone E Antr 89 D2
Port Laoise Laois 84 C2
Portlaw Watfd 84 C4
Portmagee Kerry 82 B3
Portmarnock Dublin...... 85 E1
Portnoo Donegl............ 88 A2
Portrush CC & G 89 D1
Portstewart CC & G...... 89 D1
Portumna Galway........ 87 D4
Poyntzpass AB & C 89 D3
Prosperous Kildre 85 D2

Q

Quin Clare 83 D1

R

Ramelton Donegl 88 B2
Randalstown
   A & N......................... 89 D2
Raphoe Donegl............ 88 B2
Rasharkin CC & G 89 D2
Rathangan Kildre 85 D2
Rathcoole Dublin 85 E2
Rathcormac Cork 83 E3
Rathdowney Laois...... 84 C3
Rathdrum Wicklw........ 85 E2
Rathfriland AB & C 89 D3
Rathkeale Limrck 83 D2
Ráth Luirc Cork............ 83 D2
Rathmore Kerry.......... 82 C3
Rathmullan Donegl...... 88 C1
Rathnew Wicklw.......... 85 E2
Rathvilly Carlow 85 D3
Ratoath Meath 85 E1
Recess Galway 86 B3
Rhode Offaly 85 D2
Ringaskiddy Cork........ 83 E3
Riverstick Cork 83 D3
Rochfortbridge
   Wmeath 84 C1
Rockcorry Monhan 88 C4
Roscommon
   Roscom..................... 87 D3

Roscrea Tippry 84 C2
Rosscarbery Cork 83 D4
Rosses Point Sligo........ 87 D1
Rosslare Wexfd............ 85 E4
Rosslare Harbour
   Wexfd 85 E4
Rosslea F & O 88 C3
Rossnowlagh
   Donegl 88 B3
Rostrevor NM & D 89 D4
Roundstone Galway...... 86 B3
Roundwood Wicklw...... 85 E2
Rush Dublin 85 E1

S

Saintfield NM & D........ 89 E3
Sallins Kildre 85 D2
Scarriff Clare 87 D4
Schull Cork 82 C4
Seskinore F & O 88 C3
Shannon Clare 83 D1
Shannonbridge
   Offaly........................ 87 D3
Shercock Cavan 88 C4
Shillelagh Wicklw........ 85 D3
Silvermines Tippry........ 83 E1
Sion Mills D & S 88 C2
Sixmilebridge
   Clare 83 D1
Skerries Dublin 85 E1
Skibbereen Cork 82 C4
Slane Meath 85 D1
Sligo Sligo 87 D1
Sneem Kerry................ 82 B3
Spanish Point
   Clare 82 C1
Spiddal Galway............ 86 C3
Sraith Salach
   Galway 86 B3
Stewartstown
   M Ulst 89 D3
Strabane D & S............ 88 C2
Stradbally Laois............ 85 D2
Strandhill Sligo............ 87 D1
Stranorlar Donegl 88 B2
Strokestown
   Roscom..................... 87 D2
Summerhill Meath........ 85 D1
Swan Laois.................. 85 D3
Swanlinbar Cavan........ 88 B3
Swinford Mayo 86 C2
Swords Dublin 85 E1

T

Taghmon Wexfd 85 D4
Tallaght Dublin 85 E2
Tallow Watfd 83 E3
Tandragee
   AB & C....................... 89 D3
Tarbert Kerry 82 C1
Templemore
   Tippry 84 C3
Termonfeckin
   Louth 89 D4
Thomastown
   Kilken 85 D3
Thurles Tippry 84 C3
Timoleague Cork 83 D3
Tinahely Wicklw.......... 85 E3
Tipperary Tippry.......... 84 B3
Tobercurry Sligo.......... 87 D2
Tobermore M Ulst 89 D2

Toomevara
   Tippry........................ 84 B3
Toormore Cork 82 C4
Tower Cork 83 D3
Tralee Kerry 82 C2
Tramore Watfd 85 D4
Trim Meath.................. 85 D1
Tuam Galway 86 C3
Tubbercurry Sligo 87 D2
Tulla Clare 83 D1
Tullamore Offaly 84 C2
Tullow Carlow 85 D3
Tulsk Roscom 87 D2
Turlough Mayo 86 C2

U

Urlingford Kilken 84 C3

V

Virginia Cavan.............. 88 C4

W

Warrenpoint
   NM & D 89 D4
Waterford Watfd.......... 85 D4
Watergrasshill Cork...... 83 E3
Waterville Kerry 82 B3
Wellingtonbridge
   Wexfd 85 D4
Westport Mayo............ 86 C2
Wexford Wexfd 85 E4
Whitegate Cork............ 83 E3
Whitehead E Antr 89 E2
Wicklow Wicklw.......... 85 E2
Woodenbridge
   Wicklw 85 E3
Woodford Galway........ 87 D4

Y

Youghal Cork 83 E3